BIRMINGHAM'S
FIRST BLACK *in* BLUE

**BY
DEPUTY CHIEF LEROY STOVER, RETIRED**

Copyright © 2014 Leroy Stover
All rights reserved
First Edition

PAGE PUBLISHING, INC.
New York, NY

First originally published by Page Publishing, Inc. 2014

ISBN 978-1-62838-359-1 (pbk)
ISBN 978-1-62838-360-7 (digital)
ISBN 978-1-62838-804-6 (hardcover)

Printed in the United States of America

FOREWORD

I am dedicating this book to the memory of my parents: Mr. and Mrs. Mose, and Bessie Estelle (Smiley) Stover, both deceased. They were both Christians and taught me from an early age to fear God and show respect to your parents, elders and peers. This book is also dedicated to everyone that had an impact on my life; foremost are my six siblings, from the oldest to the youngest: Mrs. Georgia Mae Ramsey, Mr. Robert C. Stover, Mr. Mose Stover Jr., Dr. Josephine S. Wallace, Dr. Norman Stover, and Mr. Albert Stover. Later on, my niece, Dr. Bessie M. Powell, and nephew, Dr. James A. Wallace, were added to the mix. We were a family-oriented bunch, a very cohesive group where the oldest one was protective of the youngest, and everyone looked out for each other. Growing up with this large group, I learned a lot about life: how to communicate with and interact with others, as well as respect the rights of others and treat others as you would like to be treated. My experience with my immediate family members and our peer groups enabled me to better handle interpersonal relationships later in life.

Secondly are all the educators that ever taught me, from primary school through college, and every grade level in between. I especially appreciate the ones that taught me during my formative years, who instilled in me the value of study, hard work, and fair play. They instilled in me that if something is worth doing, it is worth doing well and to give it your best shot. That type of attitude served me well and enabled me to become editor of our high school paper and valedictorian of my high school senior class. That same type attitude carried over into adulthood and enabled me to succeed in whatever endeavors I undertook later in life.

Thirdly, all of the officers in the Birmingham Police Department that touched my life in any way: from those that I worked under to those that worked under me during my thirty-two years on the force. Everyone that I came in contact with impacted my life, either in a positive or negative manner, and I was able to grow from the experience. The names are too numerous to mention all of them, but I would be remiss if I didn't mention a few:

Mr. Cordis Sorrell—he was not a police officer, but my boss who was instrumental in my taking the police examination, passing it, and as a result, becoming Birmingham's first black police officer.

Chief Jamie Moore, who advocated hiring colored police back in 1958.

Deputy Chief Jack Warren
Chief Bill Myers
Chief Charles Trucks
Captain Glenn Evans
Inspector E.E. Sosbee
Captain Jessie Sprayberry
Deputy Chief John Fisher Sr.
Chief Johnnie Johnson Jr.
Lt. Robert H. Boswell
Captain Clarence Mitchell
Lt. James Foy

> Lt. Gary Finley, Tactical
> Deputy Chief Roy Williams
> Captain Betty Gamble
> Mrs. Henrietta Henderson.

Fourthly, some special people who touched my life and I am a better person for their having done so.

Dr. Ocie Oden Jr., pastor of the Antioch Missionary Baptist Church, 400 Milstead Road, Fairfield, Alabama. My pastor: my confidant and my friend.

> Reverend Larry McMillian
> Reverend Willie Frazier
> Mr. Lee C. Sullivan, relative and good friend.
> Mr. Jake Sanders
> Deacon James Hubbard
> Deacon Charles Johnson
> Mr. Archie Lee Oden
> Deacon James Oden
> Mr. Michael Banks
> Mr. Greg Dawson, Sr.
> Deacon Mault Studmire
> Mr. Willie Norris, childhood friend and staunch supporter.

Last, but not least: Mrs. Joe Ann Brewster Stover—my friend, my love, my wife, who has been by my side through thick and thin for twenty-three years. She has been my greatest supporter in all my endeavors. She has been my sounding board and my best critic. She just doesn't tell me what I want to hear, but if she doesn't think something will not cut it, she lets me know in no uncertain terms. This helps me to grow and become better at what I do. She has been invaluable in assisting me in compiling the material for this book. I will be forever grateful for her dedication and assistance on this work.

Integration of the Birmingham Police Department on March 30th, 1966:
By Retired Deputy Chief Leroy Stover
Birmingham's First Black Police Officer

March 30, 1966, is a date that will forever be ingrained in my memory. For on this date, if everything went as planned, the makeup of the Birmingham Police Department would be forever changed. It would no longer be an all-white Ku-Klux-Klan-card-carrying membership organization. It would be transformed to an organization that would have at least one black on its roster, at least on paper, namely me. The inclusion of one black to its roster would· in no way change the department's ideology on race and segregation, nor its views concerning white supremacy and segregation of the races, in particular as it related to the black man. The inclusion of just one black would indicate to the public at least a cosmetic change that could readily be seen as an indication of tolerance and accommodation of a black as a member of the department, if not total acceptance, into its ranks. Prior to this time, the Birmingham Police Department consisted of a white male, close-knit organization of "Good Ole Boys" whose claim to fame for years had been the subjugation of blacks in general, and black males in particular, by threats, physical violence (which included beating), shooting (some of which were fatal), false arrests and charges, and taking of bribes in lieu of arrests for various offenses. I had been living in the Birmingham area for ten years prior to 1966, and was acutely aware of the Birmingham Police Department's record on police brutality and race relations. I had firsthand knowledge and experience concerning certain officers' actions in that regard. I recall having to drive through Five Points West at around 5:30 a.m. on my way to my job at Marshall Durbin, located on Morris Ave. and 24th Street south. Two officers would be parked in Five Points and they would stop me every morning, even though I would be obeying the speed limit. They would search my car and my person, including my wallet. They would threaten to take me to jail, but would take what little money I had. This went on for a while. The only times I wasn't stopped was if they had another vehicle stopped or they were not parked on Bessemer Road. I told my boss about it and he told me to find another route. I ended up going up 8th Ave. to 24th Street and cutting across to Morris Ave. at 24th Street South.

All my prior knowledge of the Birmingham Police Department's operations, including my experiences with certain officers, crossed my mind as I waited in uniform at the Police Academy for the unit that would take me to City Hall for the evening shift roll call. These thoughts crossed my mind: was I in immediate danger? Would the white officers try and harm me, maybe shoot me? For I was armed. Over the years, blacks had been shot and killed for a lot less. I realized that I presented a threat to their way of life. Would they consider me a "snitch," brought in to inform on the bad apples who were involved in all sorts of illegal and unethical activities within the department. I knew that not all of the officers on the force were bad. I was not afraid, but I was highly anxious to say the least. I thought to myself: I had always been kind of a first—first male valedictorian in any graduating class at my high school, a paratrooper with the 82nd Airborne Recon Company, among the first four persons of color to integrate that company in 1952 and later transferred to the 187th Airborne Regimental Combat Team in Korea in 1953. I was accustomed to danger and excitement, but nothing I had experienced prepared me for what I was about to encounter. I said to myself, "This has got to be my destiny. This is what God has for me, and that being the case, nothing or no one can stand in my way." I was aware of what Christ said in the Scriptures to all who believe on Him, that He would never leave or forsake them. I believed and trusted in Him, which gave me great consolation during this crucial time. However, my human weakness tended to cause me to dwell on the fact that I was alone, attempting to invade a racial bastion imbedded with bigotry and hatred directed toward blacks in particular, and anyone else who had the audacity to try and change their way of life, which was primarily to keep blacks in their so-called "place"—as second-class citizens, denying them basic rights as guaranteed by the constitution of these United States. My mind switched to David and Goliath and the results of that fateful encounter, which clearly illustrated the power of God and how He is willing and able to take care of His own, those who believe and trust in Him. I came to the realization that with God all things are possible, and as the Scriptures say, "I can do all things through Christ who strengthens me." With these things in mind, I resolved to go forward and see what the end would be.

THE BEGINNING

While standing in the doorway of the Birmingham Police Academy awaiting my ride to City Hall for roll call, my thoughts flashed back to my beginning.

There was nothing unusual about my beginning. I was born at home under the supervision of a midwife, affectionately called "Big Miss," probably because of her size. In the community of Sardis, whenever a pregnant woman's due date was imminent, the husband would notify Big Miss at least two to three days before the expected date of the newborn, based on the parents' projection. On the specified date, the expectant father would hitch the mules to the wagon and go fetch Big Miss. Upon arrival at the home of the expectant mother, Big Miss would settle in and make herself at home with the family. She would be provided with a place to sleep and would eat such food as the family provided. Everywhere she was summoned, she was treated as a member of the family. She was respected and loved by everyone in the community. She was the nearest thing to a doctor most families in the community had ever encountered. Midwives such as Big Miss were very necessary in the black communities at that time. Blacks had little or no contact with doctors who were all white; they relied on home remedies to cure certain diseases and ailments. The only time a person was taken to a doctor was when a disease was of such magnitude that home remedies failed to produce the desired cure.

I couldn't think of anything about the circumstances surrounding my birth or my life that would dictate or ensure that I would be the one that would integrate the Birmingham Police Department some thirty-three years later. It had to be God's plan for me. It just goes to show that God can and will use whomever He chooses to carry out His plan. It couldn't have been any one else but me. Born in 1933 on a farm in Sardis, Alabama, ten miles south of Selma in Dallas County, I was the fifth child of seven children born to Mose and Bessie Estelle Stover. Both of my parents lived to a ripe old age and were blessed to see all their children grow up to become productive adults in society. They both witnessed my integration of the Birmingham Police Department. They were both very religious and took us to Sunday school and church on a weekly basis. They taught us to reverence God and to treat everyone with dignity and respect. The concept of honesty was instilled in all of us. My daddy's motto was: if you didn't buy it and it was not given to you, then it doesn't belong to you and you must not touch it. People just didn't steal from one another. With the exception of one or two known thieves—everyone in the community knew their identity—we looked out for one another. During this time one could leave his house doors open and no one would enter and take anything while the person was gone.

You could sleep outside on the porch at night during the summer without fear of bodily harm. I recall learning my daddy's adage on stealing the hard way. I was about eleven years of age at the time, my brother Norman was about ten, and my younger brother Albert was about eight years old. My daddy and older brothers were away working in Birmingham, and the three younger boys were entrusted to the guidance of our mother to operate the farm. There was a stream of water called a branch that was about two hundred yards from our house. This stream emptied into a creek about a half a mile from where we lived. This creek was known as "mush" creek. We would gather water from the branch for washing clothes and utensils. We would fish in the branch as well as swim in the creek. We did not drink the water from the branch, because before reaching our farm, it ran through a pasture with many cattle owned by a white landowner. The cattle would drink from the stream and wallow in the water, making the water unfit for human consumption immediately downstream. About half a mile from there was a spring that fed from an underground stream. This spring was located down the hill from our nearest neighbor, Mr. Love Savage, and was utilized by him for drinking water. This spring fed into the branch, which emptied into the creek. About once a day we would go to the spring to get a day's supply of drinking water.

On this one particular day, which was around July second, we were going to the spring for water. Our cultivating the fields was over for the year; this was known as "laying by" the crops, which meant that you didn't have to plow or hoe the crops anymore that year. All you had to do was wait for the crops to come to fruition or harvest time. Most farmers would plant crops such as watermelons at such a time as to ensure that they had ripe melons by July fourth, and we were no exception. We always planted our watermelons on Good Friday, and that would ensure that we would have ripe melons before the fourth of July. Before reaching the spring we had to pass by Mr. Love Savage's watermelon patch (field). As we were walking past, we could see many large watermelons all over the field. My younger brother exclaimed, "Hey, look at all those big watermelons." I told him, "We have a field of watermelons that are bigger than those. Come on, let's get on to the spring." We proceeded on and went down a path lined with bare roots, to the spring located at the bottom of the path. We filled our pails and proceeded back up the path to where the watermelon field was located. Again my younger brother spoke up, saying, "Let's go in the field and thump some watermelons to see if they are ripe."

Back in that day, you could thump a watermelon with your finger and could tell by experience if a watermelon was ripe. I agreed by saying we would set our water buckets down and go thump just a few, and then we would go home. While thumping the melons, we realized that our younger brother had actually pulled one of the largest watermelons in the whole field. We were standing there dumfounded, trying to decide what to do. When Boo Savage, Mr. Love Savage's daughter, appeared at the crest of the hill leading a cow on a rope, she had a hammer in one hand and an iron stake in the other. She was apparently moving the cow from one grazing spot to another. Most farmers that had only one or two cows and couldn't afford to build a pasture would stake out their cows with a rope or chain. After the grass was eaten around the staked-out area, the cow was then moved to another area, and staked out again. This was what Boo Savage was doing when she happened upon us in the watermelon field. Mr. Love Savage's house was over the crest of the hill and could not be seen from where we were. When Boo Savage saw us, she began yelling, "Hey you Stover boys, what are you doing in my daddy's watermelon patch? Get out of there. Hey, Daddy, those Stover boys are in your watermelon patch." That Boo Savage was older than us; she was about fifteen or sixteen years of age. At our age we hated girls, and especially Boo Savage, because she had a loud mouth. We took out our slingshots and started pelting her with rocks. She kept yelling for her daddy and disappeared from sight with the cow. The watermelon had been pulled, so I decided to pick it up and carry it to the walking trail. I picked up the watermelon and we started to run. The melon was long and large and hard to carry. It slipped from my shoulder, hit the ground and burst wide open. The melon did not burst open evenly, but had most of the meat of the melon on one side. We each reached down and got a handful of the meat of the melon, eating it as we ran. We picked up our buckets (we had two buckets each) and proceeded toward home, running as fast as we could, carrying the water. The path was narrow, with weeds and wild flowers growing alongside it. As we ran, we lost water from our buckets. When we arrived home, out of breath and our buckets about half full, our mother asked us what happened. We lied and told her that some dogs had chased us. Mother stated that she was glad that we were not harmed, because mad dogs were prone to roam the area. Mother took our buckets of trashy water and strained it into a deep wooden bucket that was used to hold drinking water, because it kept the water cool.

About one hour later, we were playing in the front yard when we looked up and saw Mr. Love Savage riding up on his mule. We all retreated to the back yard. When he arrived at the fence in the front yard, Mother came out of the house to greet him. She asked him to get down off his mule, which he did. As we looked around the side of the house, we saw and heard him tell Mother about the watermelon incident, laughing all the while. We heard him say, "Those little devils knew how to pick a ripe one, for sure." My mother was not laughing at his joke. She called out to us to bring our asses from behind the house and come there, right then. Our younger brother, the major culprit, kept begging us, saying, "Don't tell on me, please, don't tell on me." When we reached my mother and Mr. Savage, she said, "You boys know better than to go messing with this man's watermelons, when you have ripe melons and a larger patch than he has. I'll teach you about stealing like a regular rogue. Go cut me some switches and come back and get out of those clothes. I ain't whipping you over those clothes." We took an ax and went and cut some dogwood switches. We didn't want to cut switches that were too big, nor could we come back with some that were too small, for we would get a double beating. When we got back, we stripped off our clothes, which were overalls, for we wore no shirts or underwear during the summer. Mother gave us all a good, sound whipping on our bare backsides, which took a long time to heal. From that day on, we never touched anything that didn't belong to us: a valuable lesson that stayed with us on into adult life.

Growing up on a farm in the late thirties, forties and fifties, hard work was a reality of life. My parents instilled a sound work ethic in all of their children and I was no exception. Big families were the norm, with the idea that the more children you had, especially boys, the more help you had in operating the farm, which provided the necessary produce to sustain the family. My parents were what were called dirt farmers, one step above sharecroppers. My father rented the farm long term from a white landowner, who owned everything for miles around. Our second landlord owned a general store, cotton gin, and herds of cattle and horses. The local post office was located in his business, and you could also catch Trailways or Greyhound buses there. The landowner's primary concern was receiving the rent money for the specified acreage at the end of each farming season, after the crops had been harvested. My parents were blessed in that regard, for there were many families who lived and worked on the landowner's acreage for food and shelter, and a small stipend for other needed essentials.

They were in bondage to the landowner for life, unless they actually ran away to the cities, which a lot of them did to seek employment in factories and coal mines. There were still others who were allowed to farm plots of land, with the agreement that a certain part of what their acreage produced went to the landowner. The agreement was that the landowner would supply these farmers with everything they needed to operate during the farming season, and at harvest time the landlord would extract from the farms earning what was owed to him for the goods and equipment he had supplied the farmers during the farming season. As a result of this type of arrangement, these farmers would end up with very little profit if any, and so the cycle would be repeated year after year. These types of farmers were called sharecroppers. These farmers shared what they produced with the landlord, who got his off the top and the farmers kept what was left. My parents looked out for us, in that they worked out a deal to rent the farm and never received any subsistence from the landowner. My father and older brothers took jobs outside of the farm in order to purchase the necessary items to sustain the family and operate the farm. They worked at saw mills, on the railroad, and later worked at U.S. Steel in Birmingham, while we younger boys operated the farm, with my father coming home every two weeks to check on us. In a way, the farm operated in an autonomous fashion without any landlord oversight, so long as he had the required yearly rental at the end of each year.

For me, hard work was a way of life. I would be up long before sunrise during the farming season, which was usually around 4:30-5:00 a.m. I would work in the fields, plowing and hoeing until breakfast time, which was usually around 7:00 a.m. No one would go home to eat; breakfast was brought out to the field in a basket by my mother or one of my sisters. I did get a chance to go home for lunch around 12 noon for one hour. This was primarily so the work animals (mules) could be watered, fed, and get a little needed rest. At 1 p.m. I would be back in the fields again, working until it was too dark to see. It was not unusual for me and my siblings to work fifteen-plus hours per day during the growing season. During the time that school was in session, I would work in the fields from daylight until 7 a.m., go home, clean up, and then walk to school. As soon as school would dismiss for the day, my siblings and I would hurry home, change from our school clothes, and hit the fields until it was too dark to see. This was a daily routine until the end of May, from elementary through high school.

I was blessed in that even though my parents never finished high school—my dad stopped in the fourth grade and my mother finished the ninth grade—they both wanted something better for their children. They wanted us to stay in school, get an education and graduate. Instead of taking us boys out of school during cultivating, planting and harvesting time, as most of the other black farmers did, my parents worked out a plan where we boys would work before and after school and on Saturdays. Very seldom would I have to miss a day at school during the farming season. Even though my dad was away working at U.S. Steel, we kept up this plan through junior and high school, and it paid off for me. In that way, I kept up with my schoolwork as well as my farm duties. A lot of my friends never finished high school, because they were pulled from school for weeks at a time during the farming season to work in the fields. I attended Mt. Olive Elementary, Central Jr. High and Shiloh High School, all located in Dallas County, Sardis, Alabama.

I walked to every school that I attended, with the exception of my junior and senior years in high school, during which my two younger brothers and I shared a car that we bought with proceeds from selling cotton. Our car was a new Ford, which created kind of a furor with the whites in the area. Our car was newer than the vehicles the white people were driving. We were often chased by white thugs, but they couldn't catch up to us in their old Chevys and old Fords. There was no public busing of black children to elementary, junior high or high school. The county-operated buses were for white students only. We had to walk past a white school to get to our school. The distance to the elementary school was about two miles one-way. The distance to junior high was over five miles one-way. The distance I had to walk to high school was about three and a half miles one way. I was able to drive to high school my junior and senior year. During my elementary and junior high school years, I did my studying and homework by the light from a kerosene lamp or lantern. During my high school years, we had electricity in the house, and I enjoyed the luxury of studying by the light of an electric light bulb hanging on a cord from the ceiling. I was a straight "A" student in high school while playing three sports: basketball, baseball, and track and field. I was the editor of our high school newspaper, called "The Shiloh High News and Views." I wrote my own editorials and was a member of the HI-Y-Club, the dramatic club, the school Acapella Chorus, and valedictorian of my graduating class of 1952, the only male student to have attained that honor in the history of the high school.

Having signed up for the military prior to graduation from high school, I was able to choose my preferred branch of service to enlist in. I chose the Airborne Infantry, primarily because it sounded exciting and one would receive fifty-five extra dollars per month Hazard Duty, or "Jump Pay," in addition to your regular monthly pay. I knew beforehand that I was going to Airborne Parachute Training School after sixteen weeks of basic training at Fort Jackson, South Carolina. After satisfactory completion of basic training, I was shipped to Fort Benning, Georgia, for Airborne training. This was hard and intense training. There were many who dropped out before completing the course; some couldn't take the physical punishment, and still others were afraid to jump out of an airplane. They froze as they stood in the door and were washed out on that account. After graduating from Airborne jump school, I was shipped to the 82nd Airborne Division Reconnaissance Company at Fort Bragg, North Carolina. In 1952 the army was still in the process of integrating all units in the service. The regiments in the division had been integrated, but there were specialty units that had no blacks or other minorities assigned to them. I, along with two Native Americans and a Mexican-American (Hispanic), were the first group of minorities assigned to the 82nd Airborne Recon Company, a so-called elite unit within the division.

We had a few problems assimilating with our white counterparts initially, primarily because it took some getting used to having minorities invade what was once an all-white unit. We minorities all stuck together and overcame the opposition over time, but not without some verbal and physical altercations. Out of necessity we became a close-knit foursome, Heap of Birds, Wounded Foot, Vasquez, and I. We went everywhere together. Our bunks were located in close proximity to each other. We all went downtown together. The only place where blacks and whites socialized together was at the enlisted men's club and the post theater. When we would go downtown, blacks could not sit in the white-only section of movie houses; they had to buy a ticket then go to the black section to watch the same movie. We would always go up to the window, buy four tickets, and proceed toward the white section.

We were always told that Vasquez could come in, but the native Americans and I could not enter. We would all turn around, go to the window, demand and get our money back. Sometimes if it was a real good movie, we would all go to the black section of the theater. Blacks could not go to white establishments in Fayetteville, North Carolina, so we would all go to black cafes and nightclubs.

My friends were given the royal treatment by all owners and patrons alike. They especially liked talking to the black ladies in the cafes and nightclubs. Oftentimes I would goad racist white soldiers who made disparaging remarks about the four of us into fights, because I knew that they had my back and no one could whip the four of us. My friends loved a good fight. Over time, no one dared to mess with us. A group of white soldiers down the aisle from where we were in the barracks bombarded us every evening with country music playing as loudly as they could from a wind up phonograph. Every evening we would ask them to turn the music down but they would not. We went to the platoon sergeant and talked to him about the problem. He said that he would talk to them about it. We didn't know whether he talked to the white soldiers or not, but the situation only got worse. We decided to take matters into our own hands and get back at them.

On the next Saturday we went downtown in Fayetteville, North Carolina, and bought a phonograph. We then went to a record shop in the colored section of town and bought some blues records, songs by Muddy Waters, B.B. King, and this song "Annie Had a Baby, Can't Work No More," and "Work with me, Annie, every time she try to work she had to stop and walk the baby across the floor." After making our purchases, we went back to the barracks, and before the whites could start in on us with the hillbilly music, we started playing our blues music. That irritated those hillbillies to no end. Someone in the group yelled out, "I wish they would stop playing that old nigger music over there." One in the group said, "I am going over there and cut it off." They had been drinking beer, and the group persuaded the loud mouth to go over and cut our music off. We were playing "Annie Had a Baby" at the time. We saw the individual approaching our position and we didn't try to stop him. When he bent down to turn off the phonograph, my buddies and I caught him with several blows to the stomach. I landed an uppercut to his chin with my right hand and followed with a judo chop to the back of his neck. He staggered back and started to run. With us right behind him, he ran down the stairs to the first floor and out the front door of the barracks. He ran around the side of the building, where he tried to enter the first floor through the back door. As he got between the screen door and was trying to open the wooden door, I picked up a half brick from the walk and threw a perfect strike that went through the screen and struck him on the back of the head. He fell backwards onto the ground. He was hurt, but it was not life threatening.

Someone either notified the platoon sergeant or he heard the noise. Anyway, he came outside to where we and the other soldiers were standing around the one on the ground. The sergeant asked, "What's going on? Who did this?" I explained to him how we were playing music, and this injured individual was encouraged by his buddies to come over to our area and stop our music by destroying our record player. I reminded the sergeant that we had complained to him about their loud music, and that he had done nothing about it. The medics were called and attended to the injured soldier. The sergeant said that he would have to report the incident to the captain, which he did. The incident occurred on the weekend and the captain was not present. On Monday the captain called us into his office, where we explained to him what had been happening and how it came to violence on that weekend. The captain was from California; the sergeant was from Tupelo, Mississippi. The captain stated that he was aware of what we were faced with and that he would be monitoring the situation on a weekly basis. He told us to ask permission from the sergeant to see him if the harassment continued, and if the sergeant refused permission, to come see him anyway. The captain informed us that he was not pressing any charges against us, but asked us not to resort to violence, but to report any further problems to his office. He also told us to be aware that there were individuals in the company that didn't want to see us there.

When we got back to our area, I was called into the sergeant's office, where he told me, "You're one of those niggers that likes to fight and hit people with bricks." He said, "You are lower than whale shit, and that's at the bottom of the ocean." He continued by saying, "You have a yellow streak down your back a mile wide, and your heart pumps piss." I just looked at him and smiled. He told me to wipe that "shit-eating grin off your face." He said, "The captain didn't do anything to y'all. He's one of those college-educated, do-gooder nigger lovers. I'll tell you what. I am going to give you a little company punishment for your part in this, for they tell me that you are one of those smart, uppity niggers and the ringleader of the group. Those others don't seem smart enough to start anything on their own." The sergeant told me that he was personally going to give me three weeks company punishment. He said that I would not be able to go to town on weekend passes for three weeks, and every Saturday beginning that Saturday at noon, when everyone else went on pass, "You will fall out in front of the barracks, dressed in fatigues, helmet and your full field pack. You will do this for the next three Saturdays." He said, "I will personally supervise your punishment." I talked to my buddies about the sergeant's plans for me.

They told me to notify the captain, but I told them no, I could handle whatever he could dish out. On Saturday at noon when everyone else was leaving the barracks going on weekend pass, I fell out in front of the barracks, as instructed, to wait for the sergeant. He was in his room, for he seldom went on pass or leave. He was a carryover from World War II and didn't seem to have any friends. He referred to himself as a career soldier. He would usually get a six-pack of beer from the PX and stay mostly in his room on weekends. The sergeant finally came outside with his familiar six-pack and he instructed me to go to an area near the parking lot, where there was a large, old magnolia tree that provided plenty of shade. The sergeant sat under the tree and instructed me to drop down and give him fifty push-ups. I knew that I was in really good shape physically, so I, being smart, asked him, "Which hand do you want them on?" referring to one-hand push-ups. The sergeant got real mad and said, "I tell you what. Let's just make that one hundred." I dropped down and knocked out the one hundred push-ups. I could do at least one-fifty to one-seventy push-ups before resting. When I finished, I was instructed to lie on my back with my hands and feet in the air in what he called the "dying cockroach" position. I was instructed to move my arms and legs back and forth like a dying cockroach and yell as loud as I could until he told me to stop. This went on for over half an hour, with the sergeant yelling at me louder "I can't hear you." He continued to drink beer while I kept repeating, "I am a dying cockroach, I am a dying cockroach" as loud as I could.

Finally he told me to halt and climb up the magnolia tree that he was sitting under. He instructed me to climb out on a large limb that was about eight to ten feet above the ground. Once I reached that particular limb, I was told to stand on the limb and extend both arms and begin to do small arm circles. I was instructed to rotate my arms forward and backward in repetitions of fifty each until he told me to stop, all the while yelling "I am a big ass shit bird" while he sat and drank his beer and yelled periodically, "Louder, I can't hear you!" This continued for awhile until, unknowing to the sergeant, two white ladies drove up in the parking area, parked and got out of their car. They were coming to pick up their sons who had weekend passes, and were going home for the weekend. As the ladies exited their car I saw them, but I didn't stop my yelling. The sergeant was unaware of their presence and kept yelling, "Louder, I can't hear you!" When the ladies heard what I was yelling and what the sergeant's response was, their hands flew to their mouths as they exclaimed, "Oh my God, what is he doing to that poor soldier?"

"That is a shame. We've got to report this to someone in charge." I got louder, yelling "I am a big ass shit bird," and the drunken sergeant continued to yell, "Louder, I can't hear you!" as I continued to do small arm circles. I saw the ladies as they hurried to the Adjutant General Headquarters Building, where there was an officer of the day on duty on weekends. I kept yelling, "I am a big ass shit bird" as I saw the ladies returning with the officer of the day, a captain. When they got close, the captain said, "Soldier, what are you doing up in that tree? Come down right now." I told the captain, "The sergeant ordered me up in this tree. There he is slumped at the foot of the tree. You need to talk to him." The captain walked up to where the sergeant was sitting slumped against the tree. He was groggy from having consumed his six-pack and no telling how much more while inside the barracks. The captain yelled, "Sergeant, on your feet right now. What is the meaning of this?" The sergeant got unsteadily to his feet and tried to stand at attention and render a hand salute. The captain said, "Sergeant, you are drunk." The captain asked the sergeant again, "What were you doing?" The sergeant said, "Sir, I was giving this soldier company punishment, sir." The captain asked, "By putting him up in a tree and yelling profane words?" The captain asked the sergeant, "Does your company commander know about this?" The sergeant said, "No, sir, I did this on my own to teach him a lesson." The captain told me, "Soldier, come down out of that tree. Go and notify your C.Q. that you are no longer on restriction. If you want to go on pass, you can. Tell the C.Q. that it is on orders of the officer of the day."

The captain thanked the two ladies, who went to pick up their sons. He told the sergeant, "Police up those beer cans and come with me." He took the sergeant to his office, where he was charged and turned over to the military police. I went to town, found my buddies, and told them what had transpired. As for the sergeant, he never returned to the company. He was court martialed, where he was reduced one rank and transferred to another regiment. We never saw him again. Word kind of got around that I had something to do with what happened to old sergeant T . . . ... I didn't try to stop the rumors, which were really true, for it helped our cause, for no one messed with us after that for fear of punishment from the company commander. The truth is God sent those two white ladies by at just the right time. I was promoted to the company commander's driver, and my buddies and I had no more real problems from the racist white soldiers in the 82nd Recon Company.

SKI TRAINING AT FORT CARSON, COLORADO, AND MANEUVERS AT CAMP DRUM (NOW KNOWN AS FORT DRUM, NEW YORK)

During the winter of 1952 the entire 82nd Airborne Division was scheduled to drive to Camp Drum to engage in winter exercises with the soldiers stationed at Camp Drum. The exercise was to be conducted using skis and snowshoes because of the great amount of snow in the area. The information was that there were several feet of snow on the ground with snowdrifts of up to twenty-five feet. The problem in our division was that the majority of the personnel didn't know how to ski. There were many, including myself, who had never even seen a pair of skis up close. In order to rectify this situation, the Division Commander ordered every company in the division to send one man to Fort Carson, Colorado, to attend a three-week course in ski training. After finishing the course, these individuals were to return to their units and familiarize and train the other troops. I was selected to attend the training at Fort Carson, Colorado. I was the only black in ski training at the school.

We all were issued a pair of skis and a pair of snowshoes, which reminded me of tennis rackets; only you walked on them when the snow was too soft and mushy to use your skis. They were rounded in front like a tennis racket and tapered off and became smaller at the rear. The bottom was made with strips crisscrossing to form a mesh design, similar to a tennis racket. When one put them on, it appeared that one was standing on a tennis racket with large rounded part in front of you and the handle-looking part behind you. I mastered the snowshoes right away, but the skis were a different matter altogether. To practice lying down as if you had a fall and trying to get up—that was easier said than done. I finally got the hang of it by aligning my skis parallel to each other and using my skis poles to assist me to my feet. We were taught to maintain, to care for the skis. They were made out of polished wood at that time, not synthetic materials, as they may be made of today. As a result, they had to be continually coated with a moisture-resistant wax (ski wax). This was done in order for the skis to glide smoothly over the snow. If one encountered wet and slushy snow, the wax would be neutralized, rendered useless, and the skiing would become difficult. Whenever such a situation would occur, you would take your skis off, tie them on your back, and utilize your snowshoes. We were taught to recognize when it was feasible to use skis and when to resort to snowshoes. We learned how to ski in a straight line and to maneuver on the skis, make turns, step turns, jump turns and most important, how to stop on the skis.

One method we learned was to come to a stop by turning your feet in so the skis would be gliding on the inner most edges, actually cutting into the snow. Another method we used was a kind of hook slide, where you would end up headed in the opposite direction. This hook slide would utilize the same principle of the skis' edges, cutting into the snow. During all of our ski training we would have to wear a rucksack on our backs. This was a large pack, with straps over and under the shoulders. This pack usually weighted about forty-five to fifty pounds. When we became proficient on the skis, we would have to go on a twenty-mile ski hike. This was on a laid out course, with instructors directing us all along the course; nobody could afford to fail. They didn't want anyone to fail. Their goal was to teach us to become proficient enough to train others, not to see how many they could fail.

The course consisted of areas where we had to utilize what we had learned: straight line jumps over ridges, jump turns and step turns and stops, as well as when to use our snowshoes. One important thing stressed during the training was to always carry plenty of ski wax along with your snowshoes if embarking on any long trip, for the snow consistency can change from dry to wet as you continue on, and you must be able to identify the conditions and take the appropriate action. On the final days, we would run the course without the instructors, but there would be umpires along the route at strategic points to monitor our maneuvers, such as jumping, jump turns and step turns, how we slowed down when needed and how well we stopped. If one did not do well the first time, he had to repeat the course. Nobody was allowed to fail. I passed the first time around the course.

When we returned to Fort Bragg, there wasn't enough snow to train the troops, so it was decided that we would go on to Camp Drum and train there, where there was an abundance of snow. After preparation, the entire division set out for Camp Drum by motor convoy. My company, the 82nd Recon Company, was the lead unit, followed by the M.P. units. Since the trip would take a couple of days with stops along the way, my unit would scout ahead and select areas where the entire division could bivouac (camp) for the night. On the first day we crossed the Susquehanna River and made camp north of Harrisburg, Pennsylvania. There were not enough military police to man all the intersections along the way, so my unit was utilized to assist the M.P.'s with road intersection duties. As the convoy passed, the military police would relieve us and we would leap frog ahead of the convoy, and clear and block other intersections in front of the convoy.

The convoy was not moving very fast, for we were not traveling on any interstates, but two-lane roads. The convoy was traveling in segments of approximately one hundred vehicles each. With a break of approximately five minutes before the next segment appeared, I was stationed at an intersection in a little town named Horse Head, New York. In fact, this was the only intersection with a traffic light. I had my jeep parked at the intersection, waiting for a segment of the convoy to appear. I had been there for some time when school let out. I was standing at parade rest outside my vehicle. A large crowd of children came up to where I was and began looking at me and listening to the military radio in my jeep. There was snow on the ground, but it was not too cold. I heard some of them talking, saying something about the "chocolate soldier." I then came to realization that all the school children were white and that everyone that I had seen in the little town was white. The children went home and came back with their mothers, bringing hot coffee and doughnuts. It was then that I learned that this was an all-white community, and the children had not seen a black person before. To them I was a novelty; they never tired of watching and talking to me. Whenever I was notified that a segment of the convoy was approaching my intersection, I would clear all of the children back and stop any cross traffic, so the convoy could pass through without any interruption. As I stood at attention and saluted the officers in the convoy as they passed, the children would salute also. When my relief showed up after about an hour, he was white, and I had to go and leap frog ahead to help prepare the campsite for the night. The children were sad to see me leave. They said, "Come back, Chocolate Soldier, don't go." I realized that those children didn't know anything about bias or prejudice; to them I was just another person that looked different from them.

We finally arrived at Camp Drum, with the nearest town being Watertown, New York. We spent a couple of weeks ski training before we were to engage the soldiers of Camp Drum in training exercises.

We were to act as aggressors in scheduled war games. The 82nd's objective was to drop several elements (units) behind the enemy lines, to capture certain key installations, such as supply depots and communications, while the main force attacked the enemy from the front. These were war games of course. We, the aggressors, wore special armbands. There were umpires with each group who made determinations as to how the offensive strategy was working and how the battle was going. They (the umpires) wore identifying head gear and they would assess the unit commander's decisions and action, determine casualties, and whether or not a unit had been wiped out or captured. My unit, the 82nd Recon Company, was one of the many units that were air dropped behind enemy lines during real action. It was snowing and there were wind gusts of twenty-five to thirty mph. Under normal conditions, paratroopers do not jump during such weather conditions. However, the exercise was on go, so we loaded up on the planes at the airfield and took off at zero hour. We were dressed in hooded parkas, insulated boots and mittens. Our parachutes were strapped on over all of this bulk, and our personal weapons were slung muzzle down over our shoulders, with a cover over the muzzle opening. Our packs, which we normally carried on our backs, were hung in front, attached to the parachute harness straps. All of our other equipment: skis, snowshoes, food, etc., were airdropped on our DZ (drop zone) from the same planes we were riding in. We were transported in C-119s, or "flying boxcars" as they were called, because of their shape. As we exited the planes from the side doors above the DZ, the clam shell doors would open at the rear of the planes and the cargo would be dispensed from the rear by a monorail and dropped, suspended by one- or two-hundred-foot parachutes, depending on the size and weight of the cargo containers. Several such containers could be dropped from such a plane, along with some eighty or more paratroopers, who exited the planes above the DZ.

It was snowing lightly and the wind was gusting. This made it hard to guide your parachute. As I approached the ground, my chute was swinging back and forth. My intention was to land facing forward, relax my knees, and do a parachute landing fall, either rolling to my right or left, then twisting my quick release metal fastener by hitting it with my hand, releasing the chute from my body. However, just before my feet touched the ground, a gust of wind caught my chute and swung me forward, causing me to land on my back with a thud, knocking the wind out of me. Normally you can control your chute using the risers (straps on the chute) to guide the chute where you want it to go, but in this case they were useless. Before I exited the plane, I had taken the mitt off of my right hand in case I had to pull (activate) my reserve chute attached to the harness located in front of me, in case my main chute malfunctioned. When I hit the ground, I tried to roll over on my stomach and deflate my chute by pulling on the bottom risers lines, which would under normal conditions deflate the chute. These were not normal conditions: the gusty wind of about thirty miles per hour kept my chute inflated and was pulling me along at a fast clip. I tried to turn over, but to no avail.

I tried to twist my quick release metal plate to affect my release but could not, because my hand was too cold and the steel release plate was too slick and cold. I just lay there as I was being dragged along on my back, causing a sheet of snow and ice to be forced down my back under some of my clothing. All I could do was yell "medic!" as I was dragged along the ground, covered by more than three feet of snow. Finally some medics saw my predicament and came to my rescue. They deflated my chute by running with it into the wind, and extricated me from my harness. I wasn't injured, just cold and embarrassed. Numerous others were not as blessed, as injuries ranged from fractured limbs to bumps or bruises. The jump was disastrous, but our overall mission was successful because of the element of surprise.

After about three months in the frozen area near the Canadian border, we welcomed the balmy weather of Fort Bragg, N.C., upon our return. The Korean Conflict was going on at the time and the United States was involved. If you were assigned to the 82nd Airborne Division during the Korean Conflict, the only way you could get into combat would be to volunteer as an individual. No unit from the 82nd was being shipped to the combat zone; if you were a member of a unit, say a company, battalion or regiment in the 82nd Airborne, your unit was exempt from being sent to Korea. However, individuals from those units could volunteer to be transferred to any unit they desired to be assigned to in Korea. I wanted to be transferred to Korea, because rank could be attained faster in a combat zone than in stateside duty. I was a PFC, and promotions came slowly if you were not in combat. Upon my arrival in Korea, I was assigned to the only Airborne Regiment that served in Korea during the conflict, the 187th Airborne Regimental Combat Team, or RCT, which meant that the unit had all the necessary supporting elements it needed to wage combat. It didn't have to depend on divisions for artillery, tanks or other vehicles needed for support. This regiment had all of those things. It also had the capability of striking deep into enemy territory or behind enemy lines, destroying supply lines and ammo storage, because of its airborne capability to be dropped by parachute from low flying planes. I was assigned to the 3rd Battalion L Company. This unit had been involved in an airborne operation just prior to my arrival and was short of able-bodied personnel. I was promoted to Corporal and Assistant Squad Leader. I was later promoted to Squad Leader with a white sergeant from the Army Reserves as my assistant. After the Conflict ended later that year, my unit was transferred to Occupational Duty on the island of Kyushu, Japan.

MY TOUR OF DUTY IN JAPAN

My time in Japan was interesting and informative for me. I found the people to be humble and respectful. They looked up to their elders and treated them with dignity and honor. They were considered heads of their families. When the family would venture out on foot, the oldest would take the lead, followed by the next oldest male and so on. The wives would always walk behind their husbands, and children would follow behind in the order of their importance, number one son, etc. I found the Japanese to be a friendly people who were very accommodating to the American occupation troops. Their presence near the city of Beppu boosted the economy in the area. Many of the residents were hired on the post in various capacities, making more money than they had ever dreamed of. Every barrack had one or more individuals who would clean, press and alter the soldiers' uniforms much cheaper than the laundry and dry-cleaners on the base, with one- or two-day service. All of the local businesses thrived financially because of the G.I.'s presence. The bars, tattoo parlors, and specialty shops all did a booming business due to the presence of the American G.I.'s. Beppu, Japan, located on the coast of the island of Kyushu, was a seaport city, and when ships would come into port, the city would be overrun with sailors, American and foreign. Bathhouses were great attractions for Americans and others.

In Japan there are three main islands: Honshu, Hokkaido and Kyushu, and many smaller islands. We were stationed on the southernmost large island of Kyushu. Because of volcanic activity, there were streams of hot water that flowed across the country; you could identify the hot water streams by the emission of steam in cool weather. This may not be seen in warm weather, but the giveaway is the bubbles seen at the bottom of the shallow stream. When such bubbles are observed, do not step in the water, for it is very hot. This hot water was harnessed and directed into places such as public bathhouses and private homes. A public bathhouse is a very large municipal building with a super large, sunken swimming pool-type structure made of concrete within this building. There were lockers, dressing rooms and other amenities to accommodate the public. Anyone could utilize a public bath at any time. A lot of Japanese took a hot bath at least once a day at a public bathhouse, particularly businessmen and women, as well as regular citizens. The temperature of the water in the public and private baths in homes was well over 130 degrees, in my estimation. I tried the water in bath public places and private residences, and found that I could not enter the water immediately because it was so hot. I had to ease in the water a little at a time. Once I was totally submerged, I could stand the heat. The Japanese are not prudish concerning nudity; they don't pay it any attention. Everyone in hot bathhouses, both public and private, was completely nude. You placed your clothes in a locker before participating in the bath.

Another group that made big money off the American military presence was the rickshaw' owner/operators. Downtown Beppu was about a mile from our army post, Camp Chickamauga. Once off duty, I used to walk downtown, but the majority of the G. I.'s would catch one of the rickshaws, which were always parked just outside the post gate, similar to cabs lined up at New York's airports. Some of the rickshaws were motorized, but many were pulled by an individual on foot. The non-motorized rickshaws were constructed of light material, possibly bamboo.

The seat, which could hold from two to three passengers, was situated to the rear of the two wheels. The non-motorized vehicles had only two wheels, whereby the motorized rickshaws had three wheels, two in the rear and one in front, like a tricycle. The non-motorized rickshaws had two handles, one on each side of the rickshaw body, extending from the rear of the vehicle to approximately six feet or more to the front. These handles could be placed on the ground for easier access to the seat. Once passengers were seated above and behind the two wheels, their weight caused the handles to be lifted up in the air. When the operators got between the handles and pressed down on them, the passengers' weight caused the wheels to move. The operator did very little pulling; the vehicle was so balanced that the passengers' weight propelled it forward. All the operators had to do was control it so it wouldn't go too fast, and slow it down while going downhill. That's why the non-motorized operators could trot along with ease on level ground, as well as on inclines. I tried pulling one and could do so with no effort at all. So, don't feel sorry for the operators, as I did until I learned better. He does not work hard, and it keeps him in good physical shape.

Although the Japanese were friendly and accommodating to the United States occupation troops, many of them harbored animosity toward the white soldiers, who used racist slurs towards them and generally treated them like second-class people. This was 1953-54, and Japan was only seven to eight years removed from the horrible devastation of the atom bomb that killed and disfigured so many of their people at Hiroshima and Nagasaki. They still remembered how bad they were treated by the white soldiers during the occupation after the war. The white soldiers from our post disrespected the citizens downtown, both men and women. The only places they could go downtown and feel comfortable were the bars and nightclubs. The only interaction they had with citizens was with the prostitutes that frequented the streets, and the "geisha girls" in the bars and nightclubs.

The local citizenry liked the black G. I.'s, for they could relate to how blacks were treated by the white man in America. They went out of their way to make the black soldier feel at home. Many of the decent black soldiers, those who didn't try to act like the white man, were embraced by the local citizenry. We were invited into their homes, got to know many different families, and took part in many local activities. I was a non-drinker, so I didn't go to bars or nightclubs. I went to the movies instead. They showed American as well as Japanese movies, with English shown at the bottom of the screen. I met and got to know many citizens that frequented the theater. We had been issued a handbook titled, "Japanese in thirty hours." I used this book to converse in basic Japanese. They understood what I was saying, but they showed me how to speak the words with a more Japanese accent. I made many friends by going to the theater, including three sisters who worked there. They took me to their home, where I met their mother (mama son) and their father (papa son). As a rule, the only females that had any interaction with soldiers were ladies of the evening. I and a few others that didn't frequent bars or clubs were the exception. We would be in civilian clothes, but would have to leave our shoes at the door. We couldn't wear shoes inside of the house. They would bring the shoes inside to prevent theft. The white soldiers had no such protection. Many came back to the post in uniform, but without their jump boots, because they had been stolen while they were in houses of prostitution. Those boots would be sold on the black market. That would hit the white soldiers in their pockets, for jump boots cost big money to replace.

The three sisters would go many places together: to bicycle races, to the statue of Buddha, rickshaw riding, wrestling and boat riding. During boat rides, they would let me sit up front, and they would paddle the boat. They would come to the post and we would go to the U.S.O., the snack bar and the movies. When I left Japan, the whole family came to the dock to see me off. During my stay in Japan, my unit spent a lot of time in the field training. We were required to make a parachute jump at least every three months to remain on jump status and continue to receive "hazardous duty" or "jump pay." We also made numerous jumps during training exercises. I clearly remember one training jump we made on Mount Fujiyama (Mt. Fuji) while on training exercises against, I believe, the Third Marines. In order to make any parachute drop, we had to go from the island of Kyushu by train to ASHIA Air Force Base on the island of Honshu, board planes, fly to Mt. Fuji and make the jump behind so-called enemy lines (the Marines). Japan has underground tunnels running from the island of Kyushu to the island of Honshu. We rode a train from Kyushu to Honshu through such an underwater tunnel. Because of the high altitude of our jump, one of my eardrums, and possibly both, were ruptured. I was in great pain during my descent and landing. The noise in my ears was like hundreds of crickets making noise. They kept me in a field hospital (a big tent) for over a month. My ears cleared up after about a month and a half, and I was able to rejoin my unit. After about three months, we flew back to the island of Kyushu and jumped on the drop zone near our base.

INDOCHINA ALERT: "VIETNAM"

In 1954, the French were fighting in Indochina, what we know today as Vietnam. They were driven back to a city called Dien Bein Phu, where their army was surrounded by enemy forces. The French government appealed to the United States for assistance. The wheels began turning in Washington, and our regiment, the 187th Airborne RCT, was tapped to go and reinforce the French. Their reason was that we were already in the Far East, closer to the area than any stateside unit. It was also because of our quick-striking capability. We were placed on alert to move out within thirty-six hours. We inventoried all of our individual clothing and equipment, and made three copies of each. The next day we went to ASHIA Air Force Base to board the planes that were to take us to Indochina. We checked our parachutes and boarded the planes, huge C-124s and C-1.19s. We finally took off at the appointed time for our destination Dein Bein Phu.

We were airborne for what appeared to me to be about five to six hours, when all of the planes turned about and headed back toward our previous destination. Our company commander informed us that we received orders to return to ASHIA, because the French had been overrun and the city had fallen into enemy hands. We all felt relieved, because a few hours later we would have been over our target and made the jump. It is doubtful whether our reinforcement would have affected the outcome in any way. We never got the chance to find out, and I thank God that we didn't. I remained with this unit, 3rd Battalion Company L, until I was discharged from the army in 1955. The Japanese name for paratrooper was "Rakkasan," which, when translated, means "Umbrella Man," because there was no word in their language for paratrooper or parachute.

CIVILIAN EMPLOYMENT/FLORIDA FRUIT PICKING EPISODE

My experience working in the citrus groves in Florida: After getting out of the military in 1955, I learned that several of my friends had been going to Florida each year while I was gone to work in the citrus groves picking oranges, grapefruit and tangerines. They stated that the pay was good and the work was not hard. My brother Norman was working in Birmingham, and our mother was moving there shortly. Our daddy was also working there at the U.S. Steel plant. My younger brother Albert and I decided that we would go to Florida with our friends and try our luck in the citrus groves. We left Sardis, Alabama, by car with two of our best friends, "Foots" and "Kid," and headed for Haines City, Florida. Foots and Kid had been there before and knew the highways that would take us there. They also knew the boarding house where we would be staying. They stayed at this same house every year and knew the operator very well, a Mrs. Ruby Smith, who with her husband ran the place and treated the boys from Alabama extremely well.

After a long, hard trip, we arrived in Haines City and settled in at Mrs. Ruby Smith's boarding house in the colored section of town, called Oakland. The complex consisted of one very large house with maybe as many as thirty or more small cottages. Two people were assigned to each cottage. The rent was $8 per week, and $10 with breakfast and supper. We opted for the latter. I had more money than anyone else in the group, so I paid for two weeks for everyone. Working in the groves, one was paid every week. My brother Albert and Kid were assigned to a cottage, while Foots and I were paired together in another. There were at least twenty others guys from the area where we lived that were staying at the boarding house, and we all knew each other. People would converge on Haines City from such places as Mississippi, Georgia, South Carolina and Louisiana; each group would stick with people that they knew and trusted. There were also many blacks from the islands in Haines City working on the citrus and vegetable farms. They stayed together as groups, even working in the groves or fields. Some spoke some other languages, as well as English.

There were two major citrus companies in Haines City, Florida: Minute Maid and Adams. Anyone that wanted to work had no problem getting hired. You could work in the plants where oranges were reduced to juice, or you could pick fruit or work with the irrigation crews, watering the young groves or vegetables. Working in a juice plant or irrigation paid good money, but it was a fixed salary. You were paid so much an hour and that was it. Picking fruit was a different matter. The money you made was directly related to the number of crates of oranges you picked. The going price for a crate of oranges was 20 cents; a crate of grapefruit was 15 cents and a crate of tangerines was 45 to 50 cents, depending on the size. A good picker could pick one hundred forty to one hundred fifty crates of oranges per day, earning well over $40 per day. Not every orange picker made that kind of money, but the average picker made around $30 to $35 per day, which was great money in 1955.

Another big money job was that of loader. These were the guys that loaded the oranges into a low boy, a truck that drove between the rows of orange, tangerine or grapefruit trees. These loaders punched the picker's ticket, attesting as to how many crates the picker had that were emptied into the lowboy truck. This enabled the pickers to keep up with how many crates he had picked during the day. This ticket would be turned into the crew foreman at the end of the day.

A crew consisted of twenty-five people with a crew foreman. The crew would be picked up at their place of residence and driven to the groves in the early morning, and brought back in the evening. The crew my brother and I were assigned to, "Alabama Boys," was always assigned an area next to a crew from one of the islands. I became friends with one of the men named Ted, who told me that his island was about seventy-five miles wide and one-hundred-fifty miles long. He stated that most of the money he made went to his family on the island. All the men from this island wore large knives in a scabbard on their belts while working or off duty. In Haines City at that time, there were no restrictions on firearms. Any American citizen could by a handgun. The men from the islands were not allowed to buy firearms.

Each picker was supplied with a ladder and picker's sack or bag. This was a long bag with a strap that ran diagonally across the chest and over the shoulders, similar to a seat belt strap. The bottom was open, but a strap folded the bottom up and closed the hole when the strap was hooked to the top of the sack. When the strap was unfastened, the bottom would open up, allowing the fruit to empty into the crate. One sack full would normally fill one crate. The ladder was another matter. The average orange tree was about eighteen to twenty-four feet high, unless it was in an old grove, where you would need a longer ladder. Usually a ladder eighteen to twenty feet would suffice. Placing your ladder on the tree was very crucial in picking oranges. The orange tree was almost symmetrical in shape. If you placed your ladder on the outer fringes of the tree, climbed up and reached out to pick fruit, the ladder would twist over and you would come tumbling down, sack and all. The best way to place a ladder was to turn it sideways and force it between the branches until it struck a forked branch. Then, turn the ladder until it rested firmly in the forked branch. You could then reach a couple of feet on either side of the ladder to gather fruit, and the ladder would not twist or turn, because it rested firmly on the limb. The most efficient way to pick oranges was from the top of the tree down to the bottom. You used the ladder to pick down to about six feet. You could then stand on the ground and pick the rest of the fruit by walking around the tree on foot. This was called "grounding." The trees in a grove were aligned in rows. Each picker usually picked two rows of trees at a time, with the crates located in the empty space between the two rows of trees.

Grounding someone else's trees was forbidden and could lead to fights and bodily harm, because the picker was saving the grounding for the last, because it is easier to get to the fruit and you can fill crates faster than using the ladder. It gave one a break from the ladder for a while. It was an unwritten code among the fruit pickers that you didn't ground another person's tree. This all came to a head one day when my brother Albert, who was a mediocre picker at his best, was caught grounding trees belonging to one of the men from the island. We Alabama Boys were working the trees next to the group from the island. Upon hearing a furor, we all came down from our trees and went to see what was going on. We found my brother surrounded by about twenty-plus islanders, all wielding the long knives that they wore on their belts and threatening to carve him up. I asked what was going on and was told that Albert had been caught red handed grounding trees that belonged to a member of their crew. They wanted to punish him by beating him up. I told them that there would be no punishment, but all of his oranges would be restored to the picker that they were taken from.

This didn't seem to satisfy them, and one of them started toward Albert, and I stepped in to block his way. I told him that if he wanted a fight, I would give him one. He started toward me and I grabbed him, and using his own body momentum, took him down. I had been out of the military for only a few months, and the self-defense judo takedown training was still fresh in my mind. When he got up, I gave him a fist to the midsection, which caused him to double over. When he did, I gave him a judo chop on the back of the neck and took him by the head, pulling it down while bringing my right knee up, making contact with his nose, which began bleeding profusely. He dropped to the ground, holding his face in his hands.

When the other crew saw what had happened, they started toward me. What they didn't know was that all of the Alabama Boys had guns and carried them to the groves in their back pockets every day. They were compact twenty-five and thirty-two caliber semi-automatics with a six- or nine-round magazine. We all pulled our guns, including Albert, which stopped them dead in their tracks. They realized that their knives were no match for all those firearms. We had them drop their knives, which we collected, and told them to take their injured co-worker and attend to him, and we would give them their weapons later. I had Albert turn over all of the filled crates that he had gathered to the person that he had wronged. Later that day, I took the knives back to the crew and gave them to the leader. The injured crew member, who they called Ted, came up and stated that it was a fair fight and that he was not seriously hurt, except his pride. After that we became good friends. I told the leader that Albert would no longer be working with our crew, but that he would begin working with the irrigation crews or work in the Minute Maid or Adams juice plant. All of those jobs paid by the hour, but the pay was excellent and he could make more money on those jobs than he could picking fruit, because he was not good at it. From then on he didn't try to pick any more fruit, but worked at those other jobs, where he did well.

We lived on the main drag, the entertainment street in the colored section of Haines City. There were boarding houses, stores, one that sold guns to everyone except those from the islands, R. T.'s shoe shine stand, a barber shop, the American Legion club, motel and other specialty shops and cafes. The colored residential section was closer to downtown than where we were staying. In the evening after work, we would frequent the establishments near where we lived, which always seemed to be crowded because of the huge volume of people from several states who converged on Haines City during the fruit harvesting season. A lot of families worked a circuit, working on fruit and vegetable farms in Florida, and then traveling to North Carolina and Kentucky during the tobacco season. On weekends we would go to Lake Wales, Winter Haven and other nearby towns, as well as Orlando and Tampa, where there were high end clothing stores where we could purchase Dobbs and Stetson hats, Stacy Adams, Johnson Murphy and Florsheim shoes. Haines City had two colored police officers that only patrolled the black section of town. We were not accustomed to seeing colored police officers in Alabama in 1955. We knew them as E. K. and Frazier. E. K. was the friendlier of the two. I got to know E. K. real well and we became friends. I never saw the police hassle anyone, and the arrests they made were mostly the results of fights or obvious intoxication. For many other violations, E. K. would talk to the offender and let him off with a warning.

    I spent an eventful fall and winter in Haines City and was able to save money and buy first line shoes and clothing. When the winter season ended, we came back to Alabama. Both of my parents were in Birmingham and that's where I ended up.

MY CIVILIAN EMPLOYMENT IN BIRMINGHAM

I was employed by Marshall Durbin Inc. from 1956 to 1960. I was later employed by PrattEnsley Building Supply, which has since gone out of business. During the Civil Rights struggle of the early sixties, I worked as an office and warehouse worker, as well as a truck driver. In making deliveries around the Birmingham area I had ample opportunities to view the demonstrations and the encounters the demonstrators had with the Birmingham police. Oftentimes my vehicle would be held up in traffic as the demonstrations and encounters with the police took place. Time passed, and the demonstrations gave way to verbal exchanges and agreements between blacks and the white establishment. The administration had changed from Eugene "Bull" Conner and his commission-type government to a mayor-council form of government. Political pressure was placed on this government to include blacks in all city departments, beginning with the police department. Time passed as this issue was tossed back and forth by the administration and the personnel board like a hot potato. It centered on being able to find so-called "qualified" blacks to be certified as candidates for the position of police officer for the City of Birmingham.

As time dragged on, I became aware that numerous blacks had taken the police exam and either failed to pass the test or, upon passing, were subsequently turned down by the Jefferson County Personnel Board for various and sundry reasons. The response by the personnel board was that they were not getting qualified black applicants. My gut feeling was that the primary reasons were that the applicants were students from black colleges—one was a college professor—or they were individuals sponsored by civil rights organizations. Mr. Cordis Sorrell, my supervisor at Pratt-Ensley Building Supply, discussed this hiring situation with me. We both agreed that since I wasn't a college student at the time and was not involved in any civil rights demonstrations or sponsored by any civil rights groups, I might stand a chance of being accepted by the powers that be as being the lesser of two evils. Mr. Sorrell's reasoning was that since the city was being pressured into hiring at least one black police officer, they could save face by not hiring one sent by the NAACP or other civil rights groups, but instead hire someone that had no connections to any college or civil rights groups. He suggested that since I fit that category and had a clean record, that I should apply to take the examination. I told him that I worked five and a half days a week; I didn't have time to take off from work to take the exam. Mr. Sorrell, a devout religious person, allowed me to take off with pay to take the exam.

On March 15, 1966, I took the examination for police officer for the City of Birmingham. There were several blacks that took the exam on that day. Three of the blacks passed the test and were eligible for the background check. I made the highest score of anyone taking the exam on that day, and ended up ranked number one on the eligibility list. A few days later I was notified by the Birmingham Police Department that I was being considered for the position of police officer, and that a background investigation was in the process of being conducted. Captain Jack Warren conducted this investigation. He came by my workplace and talked to me. He informed me that he had interviewed my neighbors and others that knew me, as well as my family, and he was there to talk to my boss. After Captain Warren had finished interviewing my boss, Mr. Cordis Sorrell, he called me back into the office and told me that his report would be favorable, and that he didn't see any reason why I would not be hired. He further stated that he would recommend my hiring by the Birmingham Police Department.

About one week had gone by and I hadn't heard anything concerning the results of the background investigation. I tried not to dwell on it, because I was aware that I was not the first black that had taken the police exam, and the others had all been rejected for one reason or another. I just concentrated on doing my job at Pratt-Ensley Building Supply as driver and part-time office worker. I didn't want to get my hopes too high. A couple of days later Captain Warren showed up at my workplace. I was helping unload bags of cement from a train boxcar up at the warehouse, which was about sixty yards from the office. Mr. Sorrell called me on the phone extension located in the warehouse and asked me to come to the office. This was not unusual, for oftentimes I would be called to the office to do inventory, stock merchandise, or help get out orders if there was an influx of customers, particularly if the orders contained a lot of lumber. I would assist him in figuring out how many board or linear feet each customer would need per order to accommodate the square feet they requested. This was not the case this time. I had no idea Captain Jack Warren was in the office until I walked in. His car was parked out front where I could not see it before I entered the office. I observed Captain Warren talking to Mr. Sorrell. I spoke and Captain Warren said, "Congratulations to the first black police officer for the City of Birmingham, Alabama." He then presented me with a letter of acceptance from the Police Department, and a letter of instruction to report to Thuss Clinic the following day for a medical examination.

Upon passing that exam, I was to report to the Police Academy warehouse to pick up my uniforms and equipment. I passed my medical exam and reported to the Police Academy as instructed by the letter. I was issued police uniforms and equipment and was instructed to have the uniforms altered and pressed, and to report back to the Police Academy in uniform on March 30th to report for work on the three-to-eleven shift. I was told that roll call for that shift was at 2:30 p.m. at City Hall and that I would be transported to City Hall from the Police Academy. This would be two days from the day that I picked up my uniforms and equipment. I was surprised that I was not told to report for training, but to report for work. I went back to work and showed Mr. Sorrell my uniforms and equipment. He was very happy for me, but at the same time sad because he was losing me as an employee. I told him that I would continue to work for him on my two off days, which I did for several years. That day I took my uniforms downtown to the Famous Shoe Parlor on 4th Avenue North, in the heart of the black district. I had been a customer there for years, getting clothes altered, pressed and shoes repaired. I knew the gentleman who did the alterations, cleaning and pressing. He was shocked to see me bringing Birmingham Police uniforms to be altered and pressed. He stated that he was proud to be the one that altered and pressed the uniforms of the first black police officer in the city of Birmingham. He showed the uniforms around to everyone in the shop, workers and customers alike.

MY FIRST DAY AS A UNIFORMED POLICE OFFICER

On the morning of March 30th, 1966, I was at Pratt-Ensley Building Supply at 7 a.m. as usual. I hadn't gotten much sleep the night before because of excitement. I worked until 12 noon on that day. Mr. Sorrell, a minister, prayed with me and for me before I left work to go home, take a bath and change into my police uniform. On the way home I thought about how awesome this was, a country boy from Dallas County, Alabama, about to dress out in the uniform of the all-white, racist Birmingham Police Department. Never before in the history of Birmingham had a black man worn the uniform, not to mention become a real authentic police officer in this city called "Magic." I realized that this was God's doing, and that I was just an instrument being used by Him to integrate this department. I knew that God could use anyone he chose for His purpose. I thanked God for using me. I believed that since He was using me, He would protect me.

I recalled the Scripture where He said that He would never leave you, nor forsake you. This thought bolstered my courage for the task that lay ahead. About 1:30 p.m. I went back to my old workplace dressed in my police uniform, complete with cap, badge and gun. My badge number was 365. I wanted Mr. Sorrell to be one of the first people other than my family to see me in my uniform. There were some customers in the office, both black and white, who were shocked to see me in my uniform. Mr. Sorrell introduced me as the "first real live black Birmingham police officer." He then called all of my co-workers into the office, where we all had a small celebration of sorts. Mr. Sorrell was extremely proud of me and took great delight in showing me off to everyone. He let it be known that I was his protégé. I had some time to spare, so I helped him in the office until all of the customers had been waited on.

I left Pratt-Ensley and drove to the Police Academy located on 6th Avenue South, arriving there about 10 minutes before 2 p.m. When I walked into the building there were no police officers inside. I spoke to the white civilian male who operated the supply room. He gave me a long, cold, hard stare, but did not reply to my greeting. I walked outside the building and stood on the steps at the front entrance. Captain Warren had informed me that an unmarked police car would pick me up at 2 p.m. and transport me to the police roll call room located in the basement of City Hall for the 3-11 p.m. shift. At exactly 2 p.m. an unmarked unit pulled up in front of the Academy, driven by a white Captain unknown to me at the time, but later identified as Captain Evans, who was accompanied by Captain Jack Warren. The two senior officers got out of the car, approached me and said, "Good evening, officer; you look mighty sharp today. How are you?" I said, "I am all right, thank you." They both said, "We've come to take you to your first roll call with the Birmingham Police Department." I thanked them and we all got in the car, left the Police Academy and headed for City Hall. Captain Evans told me to just take it easy, for this was something new for everyone involved. Captain Warren told me to just conduct myself in a professional manner, regardless of how others might react, for it was going to work out all right. As we approached City Hall by way of 19th Street North, I observed a large crowd of people, both black and white, lined along both sides of the street, as well as on 7th Avenue and short 20th Street between City Hall and Linn Park. I who was in the back seat of the transport vehicle, and surmised that the crowd had received information from either the newspaper, radio or television that the Police Department had hired a black police officer and that he was reporting to work on this date.

They had stationed themselves in position to be able to see at least a part of the historical event. As we got closer to City Hall via 19th Street, I noticed that the crowd makeup was predominantly white males, with a mixture of white females. This crowd was densely packed from the curb line of 19th Street North all the way up the steps of City Hall to the doors. Upon closer observation, I could make out blacks scattered through the crowd, male and female. The blacks were mostly around the fringe of the predominantly white crowd. However, the majority of blacks were on the west side of 19th Street, across the street from City Hall and the bulk of the white crowd. The predominantly black crowd stretched all the way from in front of the Greyhound bus station to 8th Ave. North. The crowd of whites, made up mostly of men, appeared to be agitated, and some were demonstrative as our motorcade drove past their positions. I could discern looks of anger and hatred on the faces of some, and curiosity on the faces of others. Some formed the "N" word as we drove past, and still others in the crowd just stared with a blank expression on their faces, yet there were still others who had that wait-and-see-what-happens expression on their faces. The looks on the faces of some of the blacks reflected pride as well as anxiety; and on the faces of others, curiosity and disbelief.

As we got closer to City Hall and the "Run-A-Round," the driveway that runs underneath the building, the crowd on the side of 19th Street closest to City Hall surged forward, and would have impeded or blocked our progress, but we sped up and entered the drive that went underneath the building. As we were traveling on 19th Street en route to City Hall, I thought about the many instances in the not-so-distant past, where unruly crowds of white lynch mobs had dragged hapless blacks from the so-called "protection" of law enforcement officials and perpetrated mayhem against them, and in some instances even killed them, while those whose duty it was to protect them stood by helpless or tacitly gave consent to what was taking place by looking the other way. I kept reassuring myself that surely this could not possibly happen in this day and time. Surely we had come too far in race relations for something like this to happen, and besides, there are too many decent people watching, and the whole country is aware of what is going on. Then my mind flashed back to November 22nd, 1963, less than three years ago, when then-President John F. Kennedy was assassinated in Dallas, Texas. There were crowds watching that day also; the whole country was aware of the event, but this did not protect the President of the United States. I remembered exactly where I was on that day.

I had just delivered some mortar mix and cement to a construction site at the Green Valley Country Club. As I was unloading my dump truck and talking to some black workers, the job foreman ran out of his trailer, which served as his office, and shouted to the white bricklayers and carpenters: "Hey y'all, they done got that S.O.B. Kennedy! They just killed that 'N'-loving bastard in Dallas." At this news, a shout went up from all the whites present. All the blacks present were stunned, myself included. I left there in shock and fear, not knowing what would happen to the country. If they killed the President, who could say that it would not be open season against blacks and other minorities? Strangely enough, my fear subsided when I came to the realization that God was still in charge and that I should put my trust in God and not man. I also remembered God's Word, in which he says: "I will never leave you nor forsake you." As my mind came back to the present, I realized that this was God's plan for the Birmingham Police Department. I was only a vessel to be used for His glory. I felt humble and grateful to be so singled out by God for this breakthrough assignment. As I was contemplating these things, our vehicle sped up and went down underneath the building. From 19th Street, the driveway continues in a circle and exits back out onto 19th Street North. This driveway is called the Run-A-Round.

MY ENTRANCE INTO THE POLICE BUILDING AND ROLL CALL EXPERIENCE

The vehicle I was in proceeded down a slight decline, and we ended up in a large open area with parking for several vehicles. It is in this area that units from the north and south patrol areas converge at shift-changing time, or any other time that a unit comes in from the field for any reason. The "Roll Call Room" was large enough to accommodate all the officers for both the north and south patrol areas on the same shift at the same time. There were no north or south precincts at that time. There was the east precinct, located in East Lake, and the Ensley precinct, located in Ensley. Unknown to me at the time, there were several units that did not come into Central Headquarters in order to make relief. Units assigned to beats that were a great distance from central precinct did not come to the Run-A-Round to make relief. These units stayed on their beats during roll call and shift-changing time. The relieving officer or officers, if it was a two-man unit, made relief after roll call by driving their personal vehicle from central precinct to the designated relief location, which was a location on that particular unit's beat.

After we parked in a marked off parking space in the Run-A-Round underneath City Hall, I could still hear the noise from the crowd up on 19th Street. I was escorted toward a glass door, through which I could see a large, long hallway that appeared to have doorways to rooms on at least one side that could be offices. As we entered this hallway, I could see that it led to a large open area or hall large enough to accommodate well over one hundred persons standing. As we proceeded down this hallway, the two captains turned and went up a stairway on the right side of the hallway that led to the floor above, which would be the 1st floor, where I later learned their offices were located. As I proceeded on down the hallway alone, I could see about eighty or more white uniformed officers standing all over the large room, which I supposed was the Roll Call Room. As I got closer, I could see and hear some officers saying, "Hey y'all, here comes that NIGGER, and look, he's wearing a police uniform and he's got a gun." Several others were chanting "NIGGER, NIGGER, NIGGER," while still others were saying, "EENIE MEENIE MINIE MO, GRAB A NIGGER BY THE TOE, IF HE HOLLERS LET HIM GO." Several other officers began pulling their weapons from their holsters, pointed them at me, and then pretended to blow smoke from the barrels, simulating that they had fired their weapons at me. Several of the officers began yelling, "Who is going to work with the NIGGER today?" Still others responded with, "If he lasts through the day!"

As I entered the large room, the white officers who had been standing all over the room now moved to one side of the room, packed together like sardines in a can. I had half of the large room all to myself. I thought about moving closer to them to see if I could push them completely out of the room. I didn't want to press my luck, so I gave up on that idea. During roll call the lieutenant and sergeants sat at a long table, but all the officers stood during this time. During roll call, some officers continued to mouth the words "NIGGER, NIGGER, NIGGER" and "Who's going to work with that NIGGER today?" Others would reply, "If he lasts through the day." I looked at the officers in charge, but they did nothing to stop the harassment. A sergeant finally called for silence by saying, "Listen up for roll call." This sergeant began calling out names and assignments with two officers to a unit. Finally, my name was called. I was paired with an officer named D.M.A. on unit #63. When the sergeant called out the officer's name, I looked over the group of officers to see who he was, but no one said anything or raised a hand.

So, I didn't know who I was supposed to be working with or where the unit made relief, whether it was in the Run-A-Round or somewhere else.

TRANSPORTATION TO MY RELIEF POINT

When roll call was finally over, all of the officers headed for the Run-A-Round to wait on their assigned units to come in, in order to relieve the shift that was going off duty. I followed the crowd to the Run-A-Round, hoping that I would spot unit #63. At least I would see who it was that I was assigned to work with, for nobody had identified himself as being assigned to unit #63 during roll call. I saw patrol units parked and others lined up, waiting for our shift, 3-11 p.m., to make relief. I saw a lot of numbers on units, but I didn't see unit #63. I said to myself, "Maybe it hadn't come in yet." While I was there looking for unit #63, the other officers went to the waiting units, relieved the officers occupying those units and drove off.

Finally the units stopped coming in, and all the officers that had been in roll call with me were gone. There were no other whites standing in the Run-A-Round with me; I was all alone. I stood there for a while longer waiting for Unit #63, hoping that I was wrong and that car #63 and my partner would show up any minute now. I had seen all of the units that made relief, and unit #63 was not among them. Unknown to me, car #63 was one of the few units that did not come to the Run-A-Round to make relief. That unit was assigned to an outlying beat on the south side of the city and never came to the Run-A-Round to make relief, but stayed on the beat instead. The relieving officers would drive their personal vehicles from roll call out to the relief point on the unit's beat and make relief there. The relief point for unit #63 happened to be located at 35th Street and 3rd Avenue South at the White Dairy building. Of course, I wasn't aware of that fact when I was given the assignment at roll call, and nobody took the liberty to inform me of that fact. Plus, my personal car was not at roll call, but at the Police Academy, over two miles away. I waited a while longer after all the other units had left the Run-A-Round in case unit #63 was late coming in. Finally, I went back inside the roll call room to inquire as to where car #63 was, as well as my partner D.M.A.

A certain sergeant, one of the three that was sitting at the long table during roll call, saw me as I came in and yelled, "What the hell are you doing still here?" I kept my cool. I told him that I was waiting on car #63 and my partner, for I didn't see either one in the Run-A-Round. The sergeant that called out assignments in roll call yelled at me, "Your unit doesn't make relief in the Run-A-Round; it makes relief at 3rd Avenue and 35th Street South."

I told the sergeant, "You failed to mention that little fact when you gave me the assignment." I continued on, for I was a little angry by now, for I could see through the little game they were trying to play. They were trying to make me miss my first shift, or at least make me late. I told this sergeant, "I don't even know who my partner is. I remember his name, but I don't know what he looks like, because he didn't say anything or hold up his hand when his name was called. It just seems like you being the sergeant would have had the decency to tell him to raise his hand so that I could see who I was working with." I told this sergeant, "How will I get over to the relief point? You know that I don't have my car over here; my car is at the Police Academy. I was transported over by superior officers." The sergeant looked at me and said, "Ain't that just too damn bad? You had better get your BLACK ASS on over there right now or you will be considered A-W-O-L. I would like nothing better than to write your ass up on your first day." He then added almost as an afterthought, "Get the hell on over there; your partner is waiting on you. If you are not there in twenty minutes, I am going to consider you as A-W-O-L." I stood there for a moment staring at the sergeant, but he wouldn't look me in the eyes. He went back to doing paper work, ignoring me completely. I stood there for a moment shocked at what I had just heard. I looked at the other two sergeants sitting at the table, but neither of them spoke up or offered to take me to the relief point. They appeared to be rather uncomfortable while the one sergeant was talking. The lieutenant was not in the room. It appeared that the sergeant who was verbally abusive toward me was senior to the other two, and whatever he said went, whether they agreed to it or not.

I decided that it was useless to try and reason with this particular sergeant. It was obvious that I had been dismissed, when this sergeant started talking to the other two on unrelated matters. I made up my mind right then that nothing or nobody was going to stop me from getting to my assignment, so I turned and left the Roll Call Room, and started back down the long hallway. I didn't know where the captain's offices were located that had brought me over there. All I knew was that they were on an upper floor, possibly the first floor. As I was walking toward the Run-A-Round, I kept hoping that I would run into one of the captains that had brought me from the Academy, but that didn't happen. I later learned that after they left me in the hallway, they went upstairs to their offices. They were of the opinion that everything was going to be all right, for everyone in roll call could see them escorting me down the hallway, before they exited up the stairway.

As I exited the hallway and began walking up the driveway leading from the Run-A-Round and on out onto 19th Street, I had made up my mind that I was going to catch a transit bus and get a transfer if necessary to get to my relief point. The driveway leading to 19th Street had high concrete walls on either side that hid me from the crowd's view, until I emerged at the sidewalk on 19th Street. As I came into view I could hear as well as see the crowd that still lined the sidewalks on either side of 19th Street, waiting to see the first colored policeman on his first day at work. There were mostly whites on the City Hall side of 19th Street; coloreds lined the sidewalk on the opposite side of the street where the Greyhound bus station was located. When I emerged onto the sidewalk, the crowd which had been in place since before I went to roll call and had seen all the police units exit unto 19th Street after roll call with no colored police in any of the units, began yelling when they saw me on foot: "Hey, there's that colored police!"

As I started across 19th Street to the bus stop located on the west side of the street, I heard the crowd asking aloud, "Where is he going? Are they sending him back home?" Some said aloud, "I know that I didn't see him in any of those patrol cars that left the Run-A-Round." Someone said, "Are those lowdown sons of bitches sending him back home?" As I continued on across 19th Street to the bus stop, I heard some elderly colored ladies say, "Child, I prayed and marched for this day." The younger colored females were waving and calling out, "'Hey, colored police!" and "He's cute." and "He's coming over here." They kept saying, "Isn't he cute in that uniform? He looks much better than those sloppy old white officers." I said to myself, "I know that I am sharp." I was a paratrooper in the Army and I knew how to wear a uniform well. I was no slouch, like most of the white officers they had been accustomed to seeing. The crowd that I came in contact with appeared glad to see me, even most of the whites present. All kept wondering aloud why was the first "colored policeman" they had ever seen in Birmingham standing on a bus stop? After a few minutes, I saw a bus coming across 8th Avenue, headed south on 19th Street. Even though I was surrounded by a crowd of admirers and well-wishers, I was able to push my way to the front as the bus pulled up to the bus stop. I noticed that the bus marquee read 6th Ave South-Titusville. After the bus stopped and the door opened, the white male driver exclaimed, "You're that colored police." Evidently he was aware that Birmingham had hired a colored police officer and that he was to begin work on that day.

I was a little ticked off because of what I had gone through earlier, and I answered him in a sarcastic manner as I said. "Yes, I am that 'colored police.'" The transit bus was almost full of riders, with the whites sitting in the front area of the bus and the coloreds occupying seats from just past where the white seating ended to the rear of the bus. There was at least one row of empty seats separating whites from colored riders. Integration had recently become law, but it was not being enforced or practiced locally on the transit buses in Birmingham. Legally, coloreds could sit anywhere they wanted to, but out of longstanding customs and not wanting to create problems with racist officials and white riders, they still chose seating toward the rear of the bus. The City of Birmingham did not have any colored bus drivers at the time.

The driver asked me where I was going, and I told him that I was going to my work assignment on my assigned beat. The driver told me to get on the bus. As I stepped up on the bus, both colored and whites were watching my every move. My guess was that they were looking to see where I would sit, in the white section or colored section. The coloreds were waving and smiling, and the whites, mostly female, were glaring and scowling. There were no empty seats in the front of the bus, and the rear area was full, but there was a row of empty seats between where the white riders ended and colored seating began, sort of a no man's land or neutral zone. I wasn't going to sit behind the whites, so when I got on the bus I stood right next to the driver. The whites gave me dirty looks, but the coloreds gave me smiles of approval and continued to wave at me from the rear of the bus. I waved back at them. The driver asked me where my assignment was located. I told him that it was at 3rd Ave.

and 35th Street South at the White Dairy building. I explained to him about being transported to the police building in an unmarked vehicle and I had no way to get to my assignment, since my personal car was parked at the Police Academy. I explained to him how my partner would not identify himself at roll call and afterward had sneaked off to the beat without me. I told him about the sergeant's comments, and how I had resorted to catching a bus or as a last resort a taxi to get to my assignment. As the bus proceeded south on 19th Street, the driver had a few choice words to say about the Birmingham Police Department and their treatment of coloreds over the years. The driver then said to me, "As you can see, my bus only goes as far as 6th Avenue South and on to Titusville. I don't go east of 19th Street South." I told him thanks and that I appreciated the help he had already rendered.

I was thinking that if he took me as far as 3rd Ave South and 19th Street, then maybe I could catch another bus that would take me close to my intended destination. I was almost certain that if I did see a police unit, the officers would not take me to my assigned relief point. They were all a part of the conspiracy against me. As the bus neared Morris Avenue on 19th Street, the driver said, "Those lowdown S.O.B.'s, they didn't want you to make it to your relief point on time or not at all. They wanted to be able to charge you with being A-W-O-L." The driver then said, "That is not on my route, and they will just have to discipline or fire me, for I am going to take you all the way to your relief point so you can be on time." My relief point was about two miles from where we were at the time. I realized then that God was working through this kind, white bus driver for my benefit.

When the bus reached 3rd Avenue south, the driver made a left turn and proceeded east toward 35th Street and my relief point. Third Avenue South at that time was a two-way street with traffic going in either direction, whereas today it is one way, with westbound traffic only. As the driver was proceeding east on 3rd Ave. South, several white women who were sitting directly behind the driver spoke out loud to no one in particular saying, "Where is he going? This is not on his route." They didn't address the driver, but raised the question aloud; even though I was sure they had heard the driver when he made the statement that he was going to take me to my relief point. They couldn't help but hear him, for they were in seats directly behind and to the right of the driver across the aisle. The bus driver spoke out loud when he said, "This colored Birmingham Police officer was not provided a way to get to his work assignment. I am going to take this officer to his relief point, for it is too far for him to walk." He further stated, "It will take me only a few minutes, and I will be coming right back this way. If anyone don't agree with what I am doing, I will stop the bus and you can get off, and I will pick you up when I come back this way." The little old white ladies' faces turned red, but they didn't say anything else to the driver or anyone in particular. The colored riders in the rear of the bus applauded the action of the white bus driver. When the bus reached 35th Street, sure enough there was police unit #63 parked under a tree by the White Dairy Company fence. There was a white officer sitting in the car behind the wheel. The bus driver pulled the bus over near the police car and opened the door. I thanked him for what he had done for me. He said, "Don't mention it. I was glad to do it." I shook his hand and exited the bus. The driver told me to "be careful, for there are some lowdown folks out there."

In the excitement of the moment I forgot to get his name. I truly regret not having at least ascertained the bus driver's identity. The coloreds yelled out of the bus at me saying, "You be careful now, you hear. There's some mean police out there who don't want to see you here." I thanked them for their concern for me.

MY FACE-TO-FACE ENCOUNTER WITH MY PARTNER D.M.A.

After exiting the bus I proceeded to the waiting police unit, approaching it from the passenger side. Prior to reaching the unit, I noticed that the engine was running. When I reached unit #63, I spoke to the officer inside. I said, "Good evening." There was no reply from the officer inside the car. I then said, "You must be officer D.M.A.," having remembered the name being called out in roll call as being assigned to unit #63. He didn't raise his hand, speak out or otherwise identify himself to me. I really had no way of knowing if the person in the patrol car was D.M.A. or not, thus my line of inquiry. Upon receiving no response from my white partner, I proceeded to enter the patrol car. I opened the door on the passenger side, took my night stick baton out of its holder located on my utility belt, and stuck the smooth end between the seat cushion and the backrest of the front seat. I had observed that my partner's night stick was located between himself and the clipboard, which was more toward the middle of the long front seat and secured in the same manner as the night stick, wedged between the seat cushion and the back rest. My night stick would be between the clipboard and me. After securing my night stick, I bent down and placed my left leg in the car and began to sit down.

Before I could get my right leg in the car, my partner, who already had the motor running, jerked the shift lever into drive and lurched forward, speeding off quickly, causing the car door to slam shut on my leg and foot. I escape serious injury, because when the car lurched forward, my backside was propelled backward and downward onto the seat, and I immediately bent my right knee in order to try and bring my leg into the car. Therefore, my right shoe bore the brunt of the door's force and not my leg. The shoe kept my foot from being seriously injured. Had my leg been caught between the door and door jamb (running board), I could have been seriously injured. The rapid forward motion of the car caused the door to slam shut with great force. The only lasting damage was to my dignity, as my so-called partner's actions caused me to sit down a lot quicker than I had originally intended.

I don't know what his intentions were, whether he was deliberately trying to seriously injure me or trying to scare me, but he failed on both counts. What he did succeed in doing was to make me mad, and more determined than ever to stick it out. It came to mind what I had heard some white officers say in roll call, "If he lasts through the day." That thought made me even more determined to prove them wrong. I was not going to flare up or start fighting unless I was physically attacked. I reasoned that what they really wanted to do was to harass me to the point where I would do something that would give them reason to fire me, using for a reason that I couldn't take it and it didn't work out. I was not going to give them that satisfaction. I grew up in rural Dallas County, Alabama, and I had experienced a lot more abuse, harassment and discrimination in my youth than they could ever dish out. I said to myself, "Let them bring it on. I can deal with it, not only for myself, but for all the others who will follow me." If they could pressure me into quitting or doing something that would be cause for termination, then I would fail not only myself but my people who gave so much in blood, sweat and tears for me to get to this point in my life.

You know, for some reason I really felt sorry for my partner and all those others who did not want me in the all-white Birmingham Police Department. I could kind of empathize with them, having been brought up in a racist environment, where they were taught at an early age to hate Colored/Negros, because they were taught that Negros were inferior to them. They had grown up hating, harassing and mistreating Coloreds/Negros as a way of life. The Police Department was used to enforce unjust laws designed to keep Negros in their place and to insure the so-called superiority of the white race. So, I could see their dilemma when they were forced to elevate one whom they considered inferior to an equal station with them, by hiring him as a police officer and integrating him into a department that had been all white for nearly one hundred years. That in itself would take some getting used to, some re-educating, some re-direction and some renewing of their minds. They would have to develop a new mind-set that would change the way they viewed blacks, which would affect the way they interacted with blacks on a personal level from this day forward. They would from now on have to judge the black man by the content of his character and not by the color of his skin. Some would make the cut and change the way they viewed blacks because of what happened that day, and as blacks would be added on in the future.

Unfortunately, there were some people with hearts where racism is so ingrained and hatred is so deep seated that real change is impossible for them. They would be forced to comply with rulings from higher courts and local governments regarding integration of the police department, but their hearts wouldn't be in it and they would seize every opportunity to thwart or delay the process. When my partner realized that I had not fallen out of the car, or had my leg crushed between the door and the car body, but that I was safe on the car's seat, he slowed the vehicle down to a normal speed. I told him, "Man, you took off like a fool before I could sit down. I could have been seriously hurt." He stopped the car and spoke the first words to me. He said, "If you can't take the heat, get out of the damn kitchen right now." I realized what he was trying to do. He was trying to force me to quit, to make me so mad that I would say or do something that would get me fired. I made up my mind right then that no redneck, robe-wearing, Ku Kluxer was going to run me off.

I later learned that this man was indeed a hard core Klansman, and that I was placed with him on my first shift for the sole purpose of him running me off by causing me to quit. It was hard for me to control my temper, so I just didn't say anything. I looked at him for a long minute and stared him down. He looked away and started driving again without saying anything else. I remembered what Captain Jack Warren had told me to be professional under all circumstances and everything would work out. Several days later, while working with other officers who were friendly toward me, I was told that the reason the sergeant placed me with D.M.A. on my first day on the job was because he was the toughest of the Kluxers on the force, and he was sure that he could run me off.

We patrolled our assigned beat. I guess it was our beat, for I had no way of knowing, it being my first day on the job, with no prior training. It was over seven months before I was assigned to the Police Academy for training. While riding along, I checked out the interior of the patrol unit, as this was my first time riding in a patrol car. Underneath the dash was a police radio, with an attached microphone that hung from the dashboard. There was a shotgun rack attached to the floorboard and supported by braces attached to the dashboard. A 12 gauge pump shotgun was secured in the rack. There was also a spotlight that could be plugged into the cigarette lighter receptacle. This spotlight could be carried in the glove compartment or laid on the floor near the radio. But of course, there was the clipboard, which contained daily activity reports, logs, incident and arrest reports and numerous other forms and papers.

The clipboard was an essential piece of the vehicle's equipment and remained with the vehicle at all times. Its usual position was in the center of the front seat, with one end stuck between the seat cushion and the back rest of the seat. We rode around in silence for a long while, with neither of us saying anything to each other. I tried to engage him in conversation by making small talk. He did not respond, so I just sat there looking out the window and waving to the people along our route. They seemed astonished to see a black man in a police uniform, riding in the front seat of a Birmingham Police car driven by a white officer. Finally, the dispatcher called unit 63's number to give us a call. Car 63's beat was in an all-white neighborhood on the city's south side. When there were two officers assigned to a unit and they received a call, it was customary for the officer that was driving to acknowledge the call by taking the microphone and repeating the unit's number. The dispatcher would then give this officer all pertinent information concerning the call: the nature of the call; participants, if any; descriptions, if any and/or available; and the address where the call originated. The passenger officer, upon hearing the call, normally picked up the clipboard, took out his pen, and proceeded to write down the information given by the dispatcher. This information would also include the time that the unit received and was dispatched on the call. The action of the second officer would eliminate the necessity of the driver having to stop the unit in order to write down the information; in this way they could save valuable time while en route to the scene of the incident.

When we received the call, D.M.A. picked up the microphone as he drove along. I, being the passenger officer, reached for the clipboard while taking out my pen at the same time in order to write down the information given by the dispatcher. As I did so, D.M.A. slammed on the brakes, coming to a complete stop. I was thrown up against the dashboard, for our unit had no seat belts. I still had the clipboard in my hand and he jerked it out of my hand, muttering something about "no 'nigger' is going to put his dirty hands" on his clipboard. He then began to write down the information given by the dispatcher. He had to ask the dispatcher to repeat the information because most of the information was lost while we tussled over possession of the clipboard. The dispatcher asked D.M.A. if everything was okay by using the code 10-04. He replied, "10-04." The dispatcher was aware that I was assigned to that unit and was checking on us. When D.M.A. finished writing down the information, he said, "Nigger, don't touch my damn clipboard again." I looked at him, smiled and said that I thought that the clipboard, as well as the other equipment in the car, was city property. I told him that whether he liked it or not, we were both police officers of the City of Birmingham. He turned red in the face but didn't say anything else as we continued on toward the location of our call.

Upon arriving at the scene of the call, I observed a group of whites standing outside of a residence. When the police unit pulled to a stop and the crowd saw that the passenger officer was black, they all went to the driver's side of the car. They began saying things like, "D.M.A. has got that nigger with him today." Some asked him why was I riding with him, and he replied, "They put him with me today, but don't you worry, he won't last very long. He'll be gone, you just watch and see." Some in the crowd were saying, "What is this city coming to, with a nigger on the police force? This all took place while both of us were still inside the police car. D.M.A. got out of the car, went over and began talking to the person who called the police, known as the "Complainant." He didn't ask me to go with him and I didn't volunteer to go. I just sat in the car and observed the crowd of whites as they milled around in close proximity to the police unit, looking at me and making comments about me. They didn't appear to be overly hostile, but curious and verbal. Some even came around to my side of the car in order to get a better look.

When I was hired, police officers did not have individual, personal walkie talkie radios they could carry on their belts. The only communication available to a beat officer was the radio in the police unit. When an officer left the unit for any reason, he was without communication with the dispatcher until such time as he returned to his vehicle. If an officer was to run into trouble while out of his vehicle, on a call or whatever, the only way he could summon help was if he made it back to his unit, or some citizen went to the car and called for him. But, if it was a two-person unit and the call was not of a serious or violent nature, one officer could stay with the unit in order to have available communication while his partner attended to the business at hand. I learned later that the unit D.M.A. was assigned to was a one-person unit on that particular shift, because calls for service in the area covered by his unit were usually not very serious or violent in nature.

After completion of the call, D.M.A. returned to the car, took the clipboard, placed it on top of the car, took the mike and informed the dispatcher that the call had been completed, wrote down the necessary information, entered the car and we drove off. While he was away from the unit, I kept hoping that the dispatcher would call, so I could answer the radio, but that never happened. I later learned that the senior person regularly assigned to a unit on a daily basis is the so-called "boss" of that unit. If a new officer is assigned to work with him temporarily, the new officer only does what the senior officer tells him to do, such as staying in the car or accompanying him on a call. If the senior officer on the shift doesn't tell you to get out of the car, you stay put. This has nothing to do with you answering the microphone or writing on the clipboard if the senior officer is engaged in driving at the time the call is received.

Within a couple of hours we received three calls, all minor in nature. Each time when D.M.A. would pick up the microphone, I would pick up the clipboard. He would slam on the brakes and jerk the clipboard from my hands. I was braced for his abrupt stop, so I was not thrown against the dashboard. He would not say anything, just write down the information. This happened on three different occasions: him getting a call, reaching for the microphone, me reaching for the clipboard, he <u>slamming</u> on the brakes, then jerking the clipboard out of my hand. I got tired of this little game, so the fourth time we received a call, I didn't reach for the clipboard when he picked up the microphone. He had already committed himself to slamming on the brakes and he was totally surprised when I made no move for the clipboard. Keep in mind that when he would slam on the brakes, we would be traveling in the middle of the street. He wouldn't have time to pull over to the side of the street. Luckily, we were patrolling in residential areas, where there were no vehicles following close behind us, or we could have caused several accidents.

We continued patrolling our beat for several more hours. I tried to make conversation with him, but to no avail. He never stopped for water or restroom breaks. Around 7:30 p.m., a little past mid shift, I asked him if this unit had an eating place and time to eat. I had seen all of the units' eating place and times and locations on their beats where they could eat. This information was posted on the bulletin board in the Roll Call Room for everyone to see. He replied, saying, "Yes, but I don't stop to eat." From looking at the bulletin board before leaving roll call, I knew that the place where this unit was assigned to eat was a white establishment on the south side, and he didn't want to take me in there, for they did not serve blacks there.

About an hour later, D.M.A. pulled up to a small service station located on Crestwood Blvd., where 5th Ave. South branches off to the left. This service station was on the right, about one block east of the Continental Gin Building. The service station was small, with a couple of gas pumps and only room inside for the operator and not more than two customers at one time. There was no food or drinks sold inside the business. There were vending machines along the wall outside the business.

There were drink machines, as well as machines that sold other snacks: crackers, candy and cookies. There was a restroom on the side of the building near the rear. Above the doorway was an old "White only" sign, so faded with time that you could hardly make out the words. When my partner went inside to talk to the operator, I made a bee line to the restroom. The door was not locked as they are nowadays, mainly I guess because it was previously for whites only and no other race of people would dare use its facilities. When I came out, they both looked at me, but neither one said anything.

While standing just outside the doorway near the pumps, I heard the operator say, "So you got that 'nigger police' with you today." D.M.A. said, "Yeah, for today. He won't last long." And they both laughed. The operator gave him some change and he went to the vending machines and got a drink and some crackers or cookies and began to eat. I took a dollar bill and went inside and asked the operator for change. He looked at me, then opened the register and gave it to me. I went to the machines, got a drink and a couple of snacks, and then I went and stood beside the passenger door of the police car to eat. I was taking no chance of D.M.A. driving off without me. D.M.A. went back inside the station and stood at the counter, where he finished eating his snack while talking to the operator. I couldn't hear what they were saying from that distance, but they kept looking at me from time to time. He never did use the restroom, maybe because I had used it first. By that time we had been working about six hours without a break. D.M.A. came out of the service station; we got in the patrol car and continued on patrol. We didn't receive any other calls after our lunch break, nor did we converse with one another. This made for a very long shift.

During the hours of daylight, people would stare at us as we drove by. Some would wave and I would wave back. Night came, when no one could see us, and I was a little apprehensive about what could possibly happen to me in the darkness. Everything worked out, and shift changing time came at last, and I was still alive and kicking. D.M.A. headed back to our relief point, parked the car, got his briefcase from the backseat, retrieved his night stick (baton) from the front seat, walked over to where his personal car was parked, got in and drove off without saying a word to me. I was left sitting in the patrol car with no way to get to my personal car, which was parked at the Police Academy. He knew that I did not have a ride, yet he drove away and left me stranded. It was about 2255 hours when he left, and I knew that my relief would not get out of roll call until before 2250 hours, and it would take them some 10-12 minutes to reach the relief point, so I just sat and waited.

At about 2302 hours, two cars pulled up behind the patrol unit. Two young, white male officers got out with their gear and walked up to the patrol car. I opened the door and got out of the patrol unit. They both spoke and said, "You're the black police officer." I said, "Yes, I am." They both said, "It's good to see you, but what are you doing still here, and where is D.M.A.? He should still be here to sign over the car to us." I explained to them how I was brought to City Hall from the Police Academy, and how I had to catch a bus to the relief point, and how D.M.A. had driven off and left me, knowing that I didn't have a ride. They both had some choice words for D.M.A., calling him a low down S.O.B. and a Klu Kluxer. They both told me that he was the worst of the bad bunch of racists, and the reason that I was placed with him was so he could run me off. They said my still being there proved that I was pretty tough and could take whatever he could dish out. They said that they would not be surprised if I was not placed with him again tomorrow. These officers told me that unit 63 was not supposed to go off its beat unless directed by the dispatcher or sergeant. They then said, "What the hell, we are going to take you to your car."

I started to get in the back seat, but one of them said, "Stay in the front seat, for you are just as much a policeman as the rest of us." I was transported to the Police Academy, where I thanked them for being so kind. They both said that they were glad to have been able to help. They told me to take care of myself and that they would see me later. Their words were "Take care of yourself, Officer."

After surviving day one, I was placed with D.M.A. again for day two. The next morning I went and bought an attaché case so I could carry my papers, as well as my lunch. I decided after yesterday's episode that I was going to take my lunch with me in case I was placed with D.M.A. again. The two night shift officers had warned me that they would probably place me with D.M.A. or some other officer who refused to stop for lunch. I had my mother fix me a lunch. She prepared a lunch for me that consisted of fried chicken, biscuits and pork chops, which she wrapped in wax paper and placed in a brown paper bag. Sure enough, at roll call I was assigned to car #63 with D.M.A. Again, he did not hold up his hand or otherwise identify himself when his name was called. This time, I had driven my own car to roll call, and when it was over I hurried to my car and drove to the relief point, arriving there before D.M.A. did. I had relieved the day shift officer and was waiting in the patrol unit when D.M.A. arrived. He didn't speak when I spoke to him, just got in the car and began driving.

It was an uneventful day. I didn't try to use the clipboard, but just sat and waved at the crowd as we drove by. On the calls that we responded to, D.M.A. never asked me to go with him, but I got out of the car and stood by while he handled the call. Everywhere we went I was the subject of discussion by the crowds. They would constantly question D.M.A. as to why I was assigned to work with him and how long I would be with him. His standard reply to their questions was: "He won't be here long." About mid shift I broke out my lunch from my attaché case and began to eat my chicken and pork chops. The aroma permeated the air in the car. D.M.A.'s face turned as red as a beet, but he didn't say anything even after I offered him some of my food. After he couldn't stand the pressure any longer, he headed for the small service station on our beat, where he got his drink and crackers or cookies. I had some change, so I went to the vending machine and got a drink, went back and placed my attaché on the car and finished my lunch.

I was the subject of conversation between D.M.A. and the service station operator, but I couldn't make out all that was said from that distance. We finished the shift with no other communication between us, and the only thing we had in common was when we responded to calls, he would get out of the car to investigate the call and I would get out but stay with the car. This routine did not change from call to call. He would use the microphone and write down the information; in other words, he did all of the work while I just had fun. The second day was my best yet. Shift changing time came, and again he left the unit before the relief arrived without saying anything to me. I stayed until the relief arrived, which were the same two officers who had taken me to my car the night before. We were glad to see each other. We talked for a while before I left for home. They were glad that I had stuck it out. They stated that I probably wouldn't be placed with D.M.A. again. They wished me well in my new career. These were the first white officers that I had an opportunity to really talk to, and I got to know them better as time passed. I found that they were not only good officers, but decent individuals as well.

After working my first two shifts with D.M.A., and he having failed to run me off, I was not placed with him again. Unit #63 on his shift was a one-person unit. I was assigned to what was known as "utility," which meant that I did not work the same unit on a daily basis. My assignment was to work on a two-person unit whenever one of the officers on that unit was off on his two days off, or for any other reason. This meant that I would sometimes work with the same officer for two shifts.

I found that the majority of the officers that I was assigned to work with were not as mean or as racist as the one that I was first assigned to work with. They, for the most part, treated me fairly well, all things considered. There were some who treated me decent when we were working alone together, but shied away from me when in the presence of their peers. There were still others who treated me with dignity and respect no matter whose presence they were in. I found this type attitude to be most prevalent when I was later assigned to the 11-7 shift, where all of the officers were young rookies. While working utility, I was assigned to work with many different officers on many different units. I felt that this was done in order that citizens both black and white in different areas of the city could see the new "colored policeman."

Working with each different officer was a learning experience. Each officer had his own way of dealing with situations. Some were gung ho who went strictly by the book, some were laid back and kind of let the situations take care of themselves. Most of them were somewhere in between. And, oh yes, they all allowed me to use the radio and taught me how to write reports. One day I was assigned to car 54 with officer E.K.M. This unit area of responsibility (beat) was primarily the Avondale and Kingston housing project and the surrounding environment. E.K.M. was extremely cool and laid back. On my first assignment with him, he beat me to the Run-A-Round and was sitting in the passenger seat when I got to the car. I just stood there, expecting him to move over and get behind the steering wheel. All of the officers in the Run-A-Round started laughing. They later told me that E.K.M. hated driving, and would make all utility men assigned to him drive the car. I was no exception, even though I had just a few days on the force. He said, "Hell's fire."—That's the term he used a lot—"Get in the car." I got behind the wheel, drove out of the Run-A-Round and headed toward Avondale/Kingston.

I knew the location of those housing projects, which were located in predominantly black neighborhoods. I didn't know the exact boundaries of our beat, so E.K.M. spelled them out for me. He said that we patrolled from Morris Ave. North to 10th Ave. North, and from 41st Street North to 50th Street North and everywhere in between. He said that we were not tied down to that area, and sometimes we responded to calls outside of the prescribed area. I drove around the boundaries that encompassed the beat and then started crisscrossing the area. I drove through the neighborhoods of Avondale and Kingston, including the housing projects. Everywhere we went, crowds would flock out to the street, waving and calling to their neighbors to come see the colored policeman.

We would stop the car periodically, and the crowd, mostly women and children, would converge on the patrol car. It was like a small parade or circus. The crowd, old and young, knew E.K.M., and he knew most of the older ones by name. He would introduce me to them by my first name, of course, and told them that I was his new partner. The persons in the crowd called him by his last name. They said, "Mr. M., he sure is cute. He looks a lot better than you do." Everyone laughed at that, including E.K.M. They crowded around the driver's side and began reaching into the car. E.K.M. said, "Hell's fire. Get back. You're going to suffocate Leroy." Someone in the crowd said, "He's my cousin, let me through." Later, E.K.M. put the word out that I had a lot of cousins in both Avondale and Kingston. He had a field day showing me around. Every call we responded to, we were met by crowds of people, mostly female. We actually would have to wade through a wall of people to get to the actual crime scene. It appeared as if the crowd knew in advance where we would be going next and they would beat us there. I believe that some calls on minor incidents were made just so we could show up.

Later on that day, we received a call on a person having been injured in a fight in the Kingston housing projects. When we arrived on the scene, there were at least three to four hundred people crowding around the apartment unit where the incident occurred. As we got out of the police unit and started toward the apartment, we were blocked by the crowd, who were pushing and shoving each other trying to see the colored police officer. At this time, E.K.M. took out his night stick (baton) and, holding it parallel with both hands, was using it to push the crowd and make a way for us to reach the scene. The crowd began to slowly move back and aside, allowing us to slowly move forward. E.K.M. yelled at the crowd, which were mostly females, "Get back, and let us through." The crowd was not boisterous or hostile; they were just trying to see and get close to me, the first colored police they had ever seen in Birmingham. I took out my baton and, using it in the manner of E.K.M., I stood shoulder to shoulder with him and began pushing the crowd.

I hadn't had any type of training, let alone riot control training. This was my third day on the job. I began yelling, "Get back, let us through!" What few males there were in the crowd yelled, "He's not a Soul Brother; he's just like the white man." We finally reached the door of the apartment where the incident occurred. As we entered the apartment, I observed blood all over the floor, on the walls, and all over the bed. A young black male was lying across the bed with a blood-soaked towel on his face. Upon closer examination, I noticed that there was a long gash that extended diagonally across his face, starting from his hair line and continuing down the side of his face, across his right eye and through his upper and lower lips. There was evidence of a violent struggle throughout the room. E.K.M. instructed me to go back to the patrol car and call the dispatcher and request an ambulance. While he gathered information for his report, I pushed my way through the crowd, arrived at the patrol car, reached in, retrieved the microphone, contacted the dispatcher, and gave her the necessary information in what I thought was a very professional manner. I waited by the patrol unit until the ambulance arrived and escorted the attendants through the crowd and into the apartment where the victim lay.

After the victim was attended to and placed on the stretcher, I escorted the attendants and victim to the ambulance, where they placed the victim inside and left the scene. I went back inside, where

E.K.M. was talking to some witnesses. They all knew the attacker by name and so did E.K.M. He was described as a black male about twenty years of age, and about five-ten and weighing around 160 pounds. He was said to be wearing blue jeans, a burgundy Banlon short sleeve shirt, and Converse sneakers. It was stated that he was armed with a long switchblade knife. After gathering all the necessary information, we returned to our car by pushing our way through the crowd of well wishers and admirers and left the scene. E.K.M. was driving at this time. He said that we would canvass the immediate area in hope that we would spot him.

There was a place not far from the crime scene where most of the black men from Kingston hung out. It was a barbershop run by Weldon Clark, a gospel disc jockey. There were several large shade trees near the shop, and underneath the trees were some old tables, some chairs, stools, benches and other items used for sitting. The men would be gathered there daily where they played dominos, checkers, cards, shot dice, and drank a little moonshine whiskey on the side. Whenever the police would show up, there would not be any whiskey or dice games in sight. They would all be standing or sitting around very innocent, watching domino or checkers games being played. They had good look-outs who would warn them of any approaching police car.

As we approached this area, I could see a large crowd of men standing and sitting around several tables, apparently watching the various games of dominos, checkers and cards being played. As we got closer to the crowd, I observed a young man fitting the description of the suspect, standing in the crowd. He was the one person wearing a burgundy Banlon shirt. As we got closer, he started moving toward the edge of the crowd, away from the direction we were approaching from. When we got within about fifteen yards of the crowd, the suspect took off running. I told E.K.M., "There he is!" and E.K.M. said, "Yes, I know." By this time we had pulled up to where the crowd was gathered. Before E.K.M. could come to a complete stop, I was out of the car like a jack out of a box and was running after the suspect. He had a distance of about twenty-five yards on me and he was wearing Converse tennis shoes, while I had on my utility belt with all of my equipment on it, plus I was wearing navy-type shoes. The only thing that I wasn't wearing was my cap, which was in the patrol car.

As I started after him, I heard some of the older men say, "That's that colored police, he's going to get him." I started gaining on the suspect as he headed back toward the projects. By the time he reached the projects, I was less than fifteen feet behind him. He ran down the entire length of one housing complex, with people coming out of their units to watch us as we went up and down several complexes, with me right behind him. No one would let him come in their doors. A large crowd followed us from one complex to another, yelling, "Get him, colored police," "Catch him," "The white police would shoot him." As the crowd followed us, they kept saying, "This colored police will put an end to this cutting and shooting out here." As we went up one row of units, the crowd would be standing out front, and as we would go down the backside, the crowd would shift to the rear of the units. It was like a parade or marathon, with the crowd cheering me on.

I was heating the suspect so hot that he left the projects and headed toward 10th Ave. with me right behind. The suspect headed west in the middle of the street. My partner E.K.M. was driving around in the projects looking for me. It was around 5:30 p.m. when we reached 10th Ave., and the evening traffic was heavy. Drivers were swerving and slamming on their brakes and blowing their car horns as we ran down the middle of the street. I am sure that they were surprised to see a policeman, especially a black one, chasing a suspect down a city street. During that time, police didn't chase black suspects; they just shot them if they tried to run from them.

As we passed Stockham Valves and Fittings and neared Tallapoosa Street, I was within four feet of the suspect. The crowd was some distance behind us, and I could hear E.K.M.'s siren even further back and heading in my direction. He saw the crowd and knew which direction I was heading. When the suspect turned north on Cahaba Street, I was within two feet of him. I made up my mind to put a halt to this chase. It seems like this guy could go on forever. I lunged for him, catching him about his waist.

My hands slipped down to around his legs, and down he went. I knew this was my last chance, for if I missed and fell down, he could gain valuable ground on me. We were approaching residential houses that he could run between and possibly elude me, so I had to take him down then. When he hit the ground on his stomach, he rolled over on his back, reached in his pocket with his right hand, and pulled out a switchblade Case knife. I immediately pulled out my night stick and struck him on the right arm as hard as I could. The open knife flew out of his hand and he yelled, "You've broken my arm!" I told him, "I'll break you're a_ _. Roll over on your stomach." When he did, I pulled both of his arms behind his back and handcuffed him. I pulled him to his feet, with him crying all the time that his arm was broken. As I marched him back toward 10th Ave., I met the crowd and E.K.M., who jumped out of the police car, grabbed the suspect, opened the rear door of the car and slammed him down on the seat. I had recovered the knife at the arrest scene and gave it to E.K.M. He told the cheering crowd, "He (the suspect) should know better than to run from my partner Leroy, for he's like a blue streak." The crowd said, "We sure are glad to see the "Colored Police.' You all are going to clean up these projects now."

E.K.M. put the word out around the police department about how fast I was, and I became known as the "Blue Streak," at least in my presence. I worked with E.K.M. two days a week for several months and I really enjoyed the assignment. The eating place for car 54 was a white establishment near his beat. He didn't hesitate to take me in there to eat, and introduced me as his new partner. I think that he got a kick out of seeing the looks on the faces of some of the customers. He told me "Hell's fire, we're police, we go wherever we want to go. If anyone tries to stop us, we shut down the joint and put them in jail for discrimination."

I recall an assignment with another officer whose beat was East Birmingham. I'll refer to this officer as J.S. He was a decent person and treated me well from day one. I learned from him that he lived on the beat we were assigned to. He was aware that I brought my lunch since my encounter with D.M.A. I did this because working utility you never knew what unit you would be assigned to prior to roll call each day. In case I was assigned to a racist who didn't want to take me into the white eating places, I would have my own lunch. As we were patrolling that day, J.S. said, "Leroy, I live on this beat and I go home to eat. I know that you brought your lunch with you today, so would you mind if I stopped by my house for lunchtime, for my wife prepares lunch for me every day."

I told him I didn't mind at all. At about mid shift we pulled up in front of his house, which was enclosed in a fence. J.S. asked me if I wanted to get out and I told him no, that I would eat my lunch in the car. As he opened the car door and started toward the gate in the fence, a young boy about 4-5 years of age ran out on the porch and yelled, "Daddy, Daddy, you're home." Then the little boy saw me in the car and started yelling for his mother by saying, "Momma, Momma, come see. Daddy has brought that nigger home with him today." The little boy kept calling for his mother to come see until J.S. ran up the steps, grabbed him by one arm and jerked him on into the house. I heard J.S. scolding the lad and him crying from within the house. J.S. came back outside to the car, got in, and apologized for what I had heard. I told him, "Don't sweat it. The child is innocent. He was only repeating what he had heard." He told me, "Yeah, you know that you are right. I discussed with my wife in the presence of my son that I was assigned to work with you today." I don't know which one used the N-word in discussing me, but I do know that after that incident, J.S. bent over backwards to make me feel comfortable. I worked with him the following day and he asked permission to go by his house. When we arrived this time, the little boy was nowhere to be seen. I guessed that the wife kept him in the house. I have a suspicion that the wife was the culprit as it related to using the N-word.

I have known J.S. from my first day working with him; throughout my thirty-plus-year career, I have never known him to be anything but a gentleman. He would always ask for me to work with him. I have never known him to use derogatory language toward or about any black person, and we encountered some tense situations involving blacks at their worst. He always referred to them as Mr. or Sir, Mrs. or Miss. We became very good friends over the years and still are. He was my boss during one point in my career when I was a shift lieutenant.

As a utility officer, I worked with at least a dozen or more officers. Some were good officers, some not so good. Some I learned later were on the take, being paid off by "shot house operators," those who sold house moonshine whiskey as well as state store whiskey illegally. When I was hired, there were hundreds of such houses operating in Birmingham, with the bulk of them run by black operators in black neighborhoods. These operators would pay the officers on whose beat they were located a fee of five dollars and up per week in order that they might operate with impunity, with no fear of being busted by the County or perhaps the Vice Detail. As a reward for being paid, these particular officers would inform the operators of any impending raids by the County and take care of any competition that was not paying off the police by singling them out for raids by the Vice Squad. In my first months on the force, I worked with officers who would actually stop by shot houses with me in the car. I was told to stay in the car and listen to the radio while he would stop by and see a friend of his. They would even sometimes bring the person they went to see back out to the patrol car to meet me. I later learned that they wanted the operators to see what I looked like in case Vice would use me in an undercover capacity to bust the operation; that way, if I was sent there to make a buy, they would recognize me and refuse to sell me anything

As I was assigned with different officers on different beats, the routine was the same. They would stop by several houses during the shift on the pretense of seeing this old boy or this old girl, but I later learned that they were all shot house operators. They went in and got paid off while I sat in the car, not knowing what was going on. I later learned that not only were certain beat officers collecting payoffs for themselves, but they were collecting for certain higher-ups in the department. Let me emphasize that not all officers or supervisors were on the take. There were a lot of honest officers on the force. I remember when I and (J.J) Johnnie Johnson Jr. (the second black officer hired) were used by the Vice Squad to try and bust some shot houses. When we would arrive at the door, the operators would call us by name and say, "I'm not selling anything."

We went to one house that Vice knew operated openly. When we parked our undercover car about two blocks away and began walking toward the house, a patrol car pulled up in front of the house, and an officer got out and went in and came back out. After that, about twenty to thirty people came out of the house and backyard and started walking away. The operator had been warned that Vice was going to bust the place that night. Later in my career, several individuals who once operated shot houses told me that the beat officers had furnished them with pictures of me, and later of the other two officers that were hired, with instructions to shoot us if we ever showed up trying to buy whiskey. I thank God that they didn't follow through with the officers' requests.

Robert Boswell (the third black police officer hired) and I were working undercover in the East Birmingham area. Vice had dropped us off several blocks from a notorious shot house, with instructions to go in and make a buy. We were bugged so Vice could monitor our transaction. We came to a house where there were about fifty to seventy-five people in and around the house, drinking beer. There was loud music playing inside of the house.

We thought that we were at the right place, but in reality the house that we wanted was about two blocks farther on down the street. As we entered the house, we saw that the people appeared well dressed, middle age and above, and well mannered. We walked up to the person who was selling beer and fish sandwiches. She was about middle aged and appeared to be the owner of the house. We ordered two beers and two fish sandwiches, and started eating the sandwiches but kept the beers for evidence. I gave the code on my concealed microphone that we had made a buy, and within minutes Vice was walking in. The sergeant in charge went to the owner of the house and informed her that she had just sold alcohol to two undercover policemen and that she was under arrest. We presented our I.D. and the beers as evidence. The lady started crying; she said, "Lord, I am no bootlegger. I am having a fish fry to raise money for my church and I was just selling a little beer and soft drinks." The sergeant said, "I'm sorry, but you sold beer to two undercover officers," and he presented us to the lady. The lady said, "Lord, I prayed for colored police." The sergeant said, "Seems like you prayed just a little bit too hard." Since there was no evidence of this being a real shot house, everyone was allowed to sign their own recognizance and were not taken to jail, but they would have to appear in court: the owner for operating an illegal drinking place, and the customers for visiting an illegal drinking place. The court fines were $25 and $10, respectively.

Later I was assigned with an officer whose initials were L.C. We were assigned to work the Titusville, Six Avenue South area. During the day we were to patrol the Titusville, Loveman's Village area. Some so-called Muslims and Black Panthers had migrated to Titusville and taken up residence there. They had instituted a feeding program for the children and were teaching them in the housing project Community Center. The patrol unit that worked that area would not patrol in the Village, so L.C. and myself were assigned to patrol the area and check out the Community Center and find out what was going on. We found the black Muslims standing on the comers of 1st Street and 1st Avenue South, selling papers. We would stop the car, but L.C. would not get out. I would get out, talk with them for awhile, buy a paper, get in the car and drive down in the Village to the Center. L.C. would refuse to get out of the police car. He hated the Muslims and Black Panthers with a passion. I would go inside and talk to the Panthers. At first the children would chant "Pigs, pigs!" when I would go in.

I kept going in to visit day after day, week after week, until the children as well as the Panthers and Muslims regarded me as their friend. The children started calling me "Policeman." The Panthers started talking freely about their feeding and teaching program for the underprivileged youth. I reported this back to my supervisors and also reported that L.C. would not accompany me, but they did nothing about it. I didn't have to buy papers anymore; they would give me free Muslim and Panther literature every week from then on.

In the evening time, beginning around 5 p.m., we were assigned to park at 1st Street South and monitor 6th Ave. for speeders. There was no radar at that time; we would just guesstimate a vehicle's speed. On this day, L.C. was driving; whenever we saw a car pass by that appeared to be speeding, we would get behind it to clock its speed. Whenever we got close enough to recognize the race of the driver, if the driver was black LC would turn on the light and siren and stop the car and give the driver a ticket. If the driver was white, L.C. would say, "Oh, they have slowed down already." I would say, "I know they have slowed down with a police car on their tail, but they were speeding." L.C. was the senior officer on the car, so what he said went. This went on day after day. I reported this behavior to the sergeant, who said the officer was using his best judgment in every situation, he was the one with experience. This went on until it finally came to a head one Sunday about 12 noon.

We were patrolling in the 200 block of Morris Ave. near Titusville. We came upon a church that was holding its Sunday worship service; all its members were black. Morris Ave. was a rather narrow street in a poor black neighborhood. The street was such that two vehicles could not meet and pass each other on the pavement, because the traffic lane was not wide enough. The church members had parked parallel on either side of the street as far off the pavement as they could get. The vehicles' wheels barely touched the pavement. Cars had plenty of room to drive between the parked vehicles. When we came upon this situation, L.C., who was driving, stopped the car and said, "I'm going to put an end to this sh_t." I said, "What are you talking about?" He said, "This fu_king parking on both sides of the street." He told me to get out and start putting tickets on all of the cars. I told him that I would not do it. I had the only ticket book that we had. He tried to get me to give him the book and I would not do it.

I told him that at the white church on Ensley Ave., they not only parked on both sides of the street, but they parked not parallel but diagonally, with the rear ends sticking out into the street. I added, "At least these people got as far off the street as possible." L.C. said to me, "You go into that church and notify them that they have to come out and move the cars from one side of the street." I told him, "I am not going any damn where. If you want those cars moved, you get your white a_ _ out of the car and go in there in the middle of service and tell those black people you want them to come out here and move their cars. I would like to see you try that." He started yelling, "I'm going to tell the sergeant you refuse to back me up." I said, "Go right ahead. You have the microphone." He took the microphone and called the sergeant. He wanted the sergeant to come out to the church, but the sergeant refused, stating that he was aware of the situation and for us to come to his office.

When we arrived at his office, he talked to L.C. first. I heard him telling the sergeant that he didn't want to work with anyone that wouldn't back him up. When he had finished, the sergeant called for me. I explained to the sergeant that there was plenty of room for cars to get through, and that the service would be over in about two hours. I also explained to him that white church attendees parked diagonal on both sides of the street during Sunday service. I then went on to explain L.C.'s racist attitude in giving tickets to only black speeders and letting the whites go. I also told how he would not even get out of the car when we were investigating the Muslims and Panthers. The sergeant said, "Well, I know, but you two have to work together, so you have to do your best to get along." We went back and finished the shift, but the next day when I reported to work, I found that I was being transferred to the West Precinct, which was the best thing that could have happened to me.

The West Precinct was staffed with officers who did not go along with the status quo, the good ole boy syndrome, who did not take bribes and who treated everyone with dignity, regardless of their color or creed. The officers at the West Precinct were considered outcasts because they did not fit the racist mold perpetuated by the Birmingham Police Department for all these years. I was welcomed at the West Precinct and given assistance in learning the ropes as it related to the workings of the department. It was from the West Precinct that I was promoted to sergeant by studying and taking notes from promotional books checked out by white officers from the police library and loaned to me, for at that time blacks could not check out promotional reading material.

UNDERCOVER ASSIGNMENT: BUYING STOLEN VEHICLES AND PROSTITUTION

Birmingham's second black police officer, Johnnie Johnson Jr., who came to be known as J.J., and I were paired together to do some undercover work. On our first assignment we assisted local and federal agencies bust a car theft ring when we posed as two hustlers wanting to purchase two expensive cars, preferably Cadillacs or Buicks 225s. These were popular cars for black hustlers and pimps. This theft ring operated by whites could procure and supply specific cars on demand, all stolen of course. We were able to convince the criminals that we were legit, pulled the deal and purchased two Eldorado Cadillacs for the agreed upon amount of cash, and assisted in arresting the perpetrators and busting up the theft ring. We worked together on several undercover assignments, including Whiskey-Vice and Prostitution.

I recall our first assignment as undercover Anti-Prostitution detectives. Prostitution was a major problem in downtown Birmingham. We were utilized to target prostitution in the colored, or black, section of downtown, primarily the area from 18th Street North to about 13th Street North, and from 3rd Ave. North to about 8th Ave. North. This area encompassed all of the black businesses, including three movie theaters, numerous night clubs, bars, other businesses including the A.G Gaston Hotel, insurance companies, funeral businesses, taxicab businesses, barbershops, cafes, shoe repair, dry-cleaning, and pool halls. During this time this area was thriving, and blacks flocked there in droves. This area, known as the Fourth Ave. Business District, became a Mini Harlem of sorts.

Blacks would converge on this area to shop, eat and socialize. They would go uptown to purchase wearing apparel from the white-owned high class stores that sold brand name items. Blacks were their best customers, for blacks bought the most expensive clothes and shoes. Blacks couldn't eat in the white establishments or use the white restrooms, so after spending hard-earned money uptown, they would come back to the 4th Ave. area to have fun. This area was a social haven for blacks, a place where they could greet friends and meet new people. Unfortunately, hustlers and pimps capitalized on the fact that this area drew people from all over that came to enjoy the food, services and entertainment. Prostitution became rampant in this area, with the prostitutes being black and the clients being black and white, so black and white undercover detectives were utilized from time to time.

My partner and I's assignment was to mingle with the crowds and visit cafes and bars in order to be solicited by the ladies of the evening. We each had a bug on, whereby the Vice detectives could monitor our conversation. We were aware that the prostitutes took their clients (Johns) to a flea bag hotel located on 18th Street between 3rd Alley and 4th Ave. North. If a deal was consummated by a price quoted by the prostitute, the prostitute would take the John, in this case the undercover officer, to the hotel. Once inside, the Vice detective would make the arrest and whisk the prostitute out a side door to an unmarked car that would pull into the alley. In order to be effective, you had to look and dress a certain way. In other words, you had to fit in before the ladies of the evening would approach you.

I was wearing a silk multicolor shirt, gabardine trousers, Edwin Clapp shoes and a Dobbs wide brim hat. My partner was wearing a multi-striped coat with raglan sleeves, some sort of trousers, and black navy-type shoes that were worn with the uniform. He was a family man and he said that his wife had made his coat. His language was proper. He did not use street jargon. He addressed the women as "O Miss" or "Madame." This terminology was not understood by the ladies of the evening. I made around eleven arrests that evening. I don't know if he made any on our first night. Over time, my partner became a sharp dresser and he learned to speak street language more proficiently. Because of our reliance on each other during the early days of our employment, our friendship grew steadily, which lasted throughout our careers and even today.

THE FIRST TWO TACTICAL OFFICERS

Birmingham's third black officer, R.H. Boswell, and I were the first two Tactical, or S.W.A.T, officers in the department. Forming a tactical unit was the brainchild of Captain E. T. Rouse. The unit's original purpose was to combat serious felony crimes: robbery, burglaries and car theft. We were to act as a quick-strike force in high crime areas. This unit originally consisted of two officers, Boswell, Sergeant E. E. Sosbee (supervisor), and myself. The unit was later expanded to about seven or eight officers, with Lt. B. Myers along with Sgt. Sosbee. Sgt. Sosbee, Boswell and I were given the task of designing a shoulder patch for the new Tactical Unit by Captain Rouse.

We came up with a shoulder patch with a dark blue background surrounded by a red border with the word "Tactical" written in gold across the top; a white chain stretched across from one side to the other about midway on the patch. A two-edged sword with a light blue hilt and a silver blade extended from the top of the patch, dividing the word "Tactical" and extending to the bottom of the patch, penetrating the chain that stretched across the patch.

Two jagged bolts of white lightning crisscrossed the sword, forming an "X." They also penetrated the chain. The chain represented the criminal element, and the sword with the jagged lightning bolts represented the swift strike force of the tactical unit as it penetrated and burst asunder the criminal element. Officer Boswell sketched the rough draft of the patch by hand. He was good at drawing and sketching. We proudly presented the sketch to Captain Rouse, who approved its design. The shoulder patch was to be worn on the right shoulder. This tactical patch, which originated with Sgt. Sosbee, Boswell and I, is still in use today by the Tactical and S.W.A.T Unit with no change to its design. I doubt if anyone in the department today has firsthand knowledge of how the tactical unit got started or its original purpose, or the designers of the shoulder patch that designates the elite unit in the department.

We worked in plain clothes and worked all hours, whenever and wherever statistics indicated serious crime was most prevalent. We were used in convenience stores to catch robbers; we would wait in the stockroom, from which we could observe the cash register and the clerk. On a prearranged signal from the clerk, we would know that the robbery was real, such as "You can have the money, just don't hurt me." We also would stake out certain businesses that were prone to being burglarized. We would utilize an old yellow cab to patrol residential areas where burglaries were rampant during the daytime, in particular around apartments and other areas when most people would be at work. On more than one occasion we had burglars carrying stolen TVs and other items flag us down expecting a ride. They got the ride they were expecting, but not to the destination they wanted. In our first month of operation the two of us made over forty felony arrests.

THE BROKEN FISH BOWL

It came to the department's attention that warehouses along the railroad tracks from 34th Street to 50th Street were being burglarized by perpetrators breaking out panels in the roll-up doors in the rear of the buildings that faced the tracks. Patrol units could check the front of these buildings but did not have access to the rear. The only way the rear could be checked was for someone to actually walk the railroad tracks and physically check the rear of each warehouse. Boswell and I were assigned this task, working the night shift from 8:30 p.m. to 4:30 a.m. We worked this area for about one month. During this time we came upon several burglaries in progress and arrested the suspects. We found other businesses where the suspects had entered, taken valuable items, stacked them outside and left to bring their vehicle as close as they could get it to the warehouse so they could load the items. Needless to say, they were arrested and the goods recovered.

At one warehouse we found twelve to fifteen expensive office machines stacked outside. As we looked, the burglar began emerging through the entrance hole with another machine. He saw us and ducked back inside of the building. Boswell stood watch over the machines while I took off after the burglar. I followed him up a stairway to the second floor. He ran to an area where there were offices on the first floor; the ceiling was no longer wood but was hung acoustical tile, laid in a metal framework. The burglar tried to cross this area to reach the wood ceiling floor again, trying to run on the narrow strips of metal, but he lost his footing and crashed through the hung tile panels to the floor below, hitting a desk as he fell. I didn't want him to get away, so I took the same route by trying to hang on to the metal framework and drop to the floor. My hands slipped and I came crashing down on top of a desk, hitting a fish bowl and knocking it to the floor, breaking the bowl and scattering some expensive fish. Boswell, hearing the noise, came running in and we apprehended the suspect. I told Boswell to get a metal trash can and we collected the fish and poured water into the can, and then placed the fish in the can. The fish did live. When the owner came to the scene he was grateful that we had saved the expensive machines; I think they were IBM machines. After surveying the damage to the ceiling and office, he said, "That damn burglar wrecked this office." He didn't notice that I had white tile chalk on my clothes also. Needless to say, all the damage was attributed to the burglar. The owner wrote a letter of commendation to the department on our behalf.

THE FIGHT ON THE RAILROAD TRACKS

One night as we were patrolling the railroad tracks in about what would be 43rd Street South, we observed in the distance what appeared to be two figures on the tracks.

When we got closer we could see that it was a man and a woman struggling. Before we could reach them, the man took up a large object, possibly a rock, and struck the woman on the head. She fell down on the ground between the tracks. We rushed up, identified ourselves as police officers, and arrested the man. Officer Boswell handcuffed the man and I looked after the victim, who was semi-conscious. I called for the medics and an ambulance and instructed them as to how to get to our location. About this time we saw the light of a train approaching in the distance, and we realized that we had to get the victim off the tracks. I called for Boswell to assist me in moving the victim to a safe location between the two sets of tracks. As we were moving the victim, the man took off, running with his hands handcuffed behind his back. After placing the victim in a safe place, Officer Boswell took out his weapon and fired off a couple of rounds at the fleeing suspect. I yelled at Boswell:

"Don't shoot that handcuffed man, Stay here until the ambulance arrives. I'm going to catch him." I was known as "The Blue Streak." I took off up the tracks after him.

The suspect left the tracks and headed toward a cluster of shotgun row houses located a short distance from the tracks. While running through the back yard of these houses, I saw the suspect start bending over real low. It was dark and I couldn't see why he was doing this. I said to myself, "Boy, he's really getting down." As I entered the back yard and the suspect was running between the houses, a metal clothesline caught me on my neck and threw me over backward. Then it came to me why the suspect was bending over. He lived in the area and was familiar with those clotheslines in the back yards. I picked myself up off the ground and continued between the houses. I saw the suspect trying to climb a steep embankment in front of the houses. Because his hands were handcuffed behind his back, he would lose his footing; every time he got near the top of the embankment, he would slide back down to the bottom. I ran up to him and grabbed him by the handcuffs and yanked him back down to level ground, and marched him back to the crime scene, where Boswell and the medics were. The department did not have a shooting policy at that time. You could fire your weapon for any reason you deemed necessary. You didn't have to report firing your weapon. I was just thankful that the suspect was not struck and that things turned out all right. I was hoarse from that clothesline for a day or two.

I WAS SET AFIRE ON THE RAILROAD TRACKS

One night as we started out on foot patrol, it was very warm, around 70 degrees. I told Boswell that I was going to leave my coat in the car, for it was too much trouble to carry it along and not need it. Boswell said that he heard on the news that the temperature would drop some 40 degrees overnight. I didn't believe him and told him so. He took his coat with him. During the night, the temperature continued to drop until around three o'clock a.m.; the reading was 37 degrees. I was almost freezing and we couldn't go back to the car until the shift was over. We came upon a pile of clear plastic behind a warehouse and I wrapped myself in plastic and tied a cord around it to keep it in place. The only opening was for my gun and flashlight. I felt that I could make it, since we only had a couple of hours left in the shift.

We came upon a 65-gallon drum with a lighted fire burning in it, located on the side of the railroad tracks. It was possibly used by vagrants, but there was no one around it at the time. We went over to warm ourselves. As we were standing around the fire, I turned around so my backside could get warm. Evidently I was too close to the drum, for I heard a "WHOOP" sound and Boswell yelled, "You are on fire!" I moved away from the fire real fast. I couldn't rip the plastic off, for it was tied on, so I hit the ground and rolled as Boswell and I continued to snuff out the flames. I was not burned—only my eyebrows were slightly singed. The plastic really flamed up, unlike the polyurethane of today, which melts when it catches fire. Believe me, I never messed with plastic again, and from then on I took my coat.

THE SWIMMING POOL INCIDENT

As members of the Tactical Unit, Boswell and I were assigned to Swimming Pool Security. All swimming pools in Birmingham were closed when integration became law, to prevent blacks from integrating previously all-white pools. After much legal wrangling, the administration decided to re-open all swimming pools within the city to everyone, regardless of race. The pools were set to open on a particular Monday. During the week prior to the opening of the pools, Boswell and I were assigned the duty of providing security for all pools within the city. Our job was to check each pool regularly to prevent vandalism and to ensure that nothing had been tampered with. We were looking for cut security fences, explosives and general vandalism.

On the Sunday morning prior to the pools opening on Monday, we were checking the pool at Collegeville when we received a dispatch that the fence had been breached and that there were forty to fifty males illegally swimming in the pool at Avondale projects. We were in separate units, #93 and #99 respectively, and we proceeded to that location with haste. As we approached the scene we observed a large crowd of black males in the pool playing around. We also observed that the fence around the pool had been cut, providing easy access to the pool. There was a large pile of clothing, including shoes and caps by the access hole in the fence. The majority of the participants in the pool were nude, having left their clothes outside the fences, and did not have on bathing trunks.

As we approached the scene, everyone left the pool and exited the fence and took off running toward the housing projects. They were stark naked because no one paused to retrieve any clothes. They ranged in ages from 4 or 5 years to about 25 or 30 years. I radioed to Boswell for us to get out of our cars and apprehend at least one of the older suspects. I got out of my vehicle, but Boswell continued to drive among those running, yelling out of the car, "Police, stop!" Nobody paid him any attention, but kept running toward the projects. Needless to say, he did not arrest anyone; everyone that he was chasing in his car escaped into the projects.

I singled out one older guy who was running down the railroad tracks from the scene, headed toward 41st Street. I took off after him, and after some time gained on him to within several feet. He looked back to see how close I was to him, and when he did he stomped his right foot on a cross tie, breaking his big toe. He fell on the slag and cross ties between the tracks, yelling, "I've broken my toe." I helped him up; he was buck naked. I handcuffed him and marched him back to the scene. Boswell was back at the scene, empty-handed of course. We learned that the suspect's name was Felix U—and that he was 28 years of age. He indicated that he was the oldest one in the group and admitted to cutting the fence lying by the pile of clothes. Felix described his clothes, and as we were looking for them in the pile, three little old ladies came walking up the path that passed right by the pool. It was almost 11 a.m. and they were on their way to church. They stopped and began staring at the suspect, Felix U—, who, being naked, turned and tried to hide his private parts from the little old ladies. As he turned they moved off the path to see better.

I was still looking for Felix's clothing and Boswell told the ladies to move on, saying, "This is police business." The little old ladies told him, "Don't you get smart with us, boy, we're just looking so we can see if we know him so we can tell his folks that you've got him." Not once did the little old ladies look at his face; they were too busy looking at his other parts. I found his clothes and he put them on, and only then did the little old ladies go on their way to church. Felix U—was charged with vandalism and destruction of city property. We were instructed to turn all the clothing in to the property room with notations to any parent that identified clothing as belonging to their children, the clothes would be released to them, and no juveniles would be charged.

COLLEGEVILLE ASSIGNMENT

As members of the Tactical Unit, which consisted of Officer Boswell and me, we were assigned to work the Collegeville, Fairmont-Riggins area. This area, which included the housing projects in Collegeville and Riggins, was infamous for murder, shootings, robberies, physical assaults and other assorted crimes. At the time we began working the area, it was so bad that the patrol unit that was responsible for that area coverage seldom if ever patrolled in the area. The patrol unit that used to patrol the area would only go as far as the service station at 26th Street and 25th Ave. North. In case we made arrests, we would have to transport our prisoners from wherever they were arrested to the pick-up point on 26th Street. We began arresting so many suspects, up to three to four at a time, that we were instructed to call for a paddy wagon to meet us at the pick-up location.

This came to a head one evening when we arrested seven suspects at one time. Since no patrol unit except ours was assigned to that area, we had to devise a method to transport all seven prisoners to the pick-up point, over a mile away. We placed three prisoners in the front seat (the unit was an old Ford four-door with long bench seats front and rear), and we placed four prisoners in the rear of the vehicle. We handcuffed the right hand of each prisoner on the outermost passenger side of each seat, and handcuffed the left hand of the prisoner on the driver's side of each seat, thus holding the prisoners that were in the middle in place by the two handcuffed arms of the prisoners. Boswell had the prisoners on the back seat move toward the driver's side of the car, which made a little room for him to squeeze in. His gun was on his right side, out of reach of the prisoners. I moved my utility belt around so my weapon was on my left side, out of the prisoners' reach. I had them move over and I squeezed in behind the wheel.

We drove slowly to the pickup point, where the paddy wagon was waiting for us. Once our supervisor found out what had occurred, he called us in and told us how dangerous it was to transport that many prisoners at one time. We explained to him that we had a volatile situation (a fight) and we had to get the participants out of the area in a hurry. Later that evening we were told to bring our car in and check out a paddy wagon, which we did. Being assigned a paddy wagon was a blessing in disguise. First, the wagon offered more protection from bullets and thrown objects. The wagon was constructed of thick aluminum with small windows covered with bars. Second, it enabled us to more easily secure arrested suspects until such time as they were transported to jail. Thirdly, it acted as deterrent to other criminals and law violators as they observed their "homies" being driven around in the neighborhoods locked up. Fourth, we utilized the wagon to convey the elderly to and from the bank in North Birmingham and local grocery stores in the area on "check day," the first and third day of each month. Prior to this, the elderly who didn't have access to a car were afraid to walk to the bank or local stores to get food and cash their checks, for they would be robbed by thugs on their way back home.

Many of the elderly became more confident because of our presence and began venturing out of their houses, walking around and sitting on porches and in their yards. They told us that they no longer felt like prisoners in their own homes. Prior to our assignment in the area, murder and shooting were commonplace occurrences. The law-abiding citizens in the area were afraid to report crimes or come forward with information that could lead to an arrest of the guilty for fear of retaliation.

We gained their confidence by telling them that no one could know who called if it were done from the privacy of their home, and we let them know that we were there to clean up the area of criminals. We used a zero tolerance method. We stopped vehicles for minor violations and called in the subjects and vehicle license through NCIC. We received hits on both the subjects and vehicles by this method and made many legal arrests. We learned from the law-abiding citizens that criminals who didn't live in the area would park stolen vehicles and use them in other crimes in the projects during the daytime and utilize those vehicles at night. The citizens who had previously been afraid began pointing out those vehicles to us. We pulled in abandoned cars and recovered many stolen vehicles in the process.

Collegeville is surrounded on all sides by railroad tracks, and there were instances where victims were shot or seriously injured and paramedics could not reach them in time because all arteries into and out of the area were blocked by trains and the victims subsequently died. We notified the dispatcher of the problem and were told that there was a law that says a train cannot sit still and block a street for more than fifteen minutes—the train had to be moving. We were told that if we found a train to be in violation, we were to walk up the tracks and write the conductor a citation. We only had to write one citation and the message got around to the railroad lines. After we had been in Collegeville for awhile, citizens were no longer afraid to go about their daily activities or report criminal activity because they were no longer afraid of reprisals from the criminal elements. Because of our presence, Collegeville and the nearby environs became a much safer and livable place for the law-abiding citizens, and a place to be avoided by the criminal element.

THE GOODYEAR STORE HEIST

I was working with Officer Boswell as the Tactical Anti/Burglary detail. Late on this particular day we checked the Goodyear Tire and Appliance store on 21st Street at 7th Avenue South We noticed that a panel was missing from the wooden roll-up door to one of the bays. Upon closer examination, we found that the door had been unlocked. Whoever had knocked the panel out had reached in and unlocked the door. We pushed the now unlocked door up, entered and realized that the place had been burglarized, and many tires and other appliances had been taken. Upon further checking, we realized that one of the two delivery vans was missing. The thieves had used the store's truck to haul away the stolen goods. We realized that the burglary had to have occurred within the past couple of hours, for the store was open for business until about 5 p.m. and it was now almost 8 p.m., but not yet dark, because it was summertime. We felt that they were somewhere in the area laying low, waiting for it to get dark before trying to dispose of the goods and the truck.

We notified communications and began looking for the stolen truck and goods. We checked all streets in the nearby residential area, including the Southtown housing projects. We then decided to double back and check all of the alleys within about a twenty-block area of the crime scene. As we checked one particular alley, we observed part of a white panel van backed up behind a particular residence. The vehicle was backed in beside a large tree located in the back yard of the house. The tree's limbs prevented it from being seen from the street, and you had to be looking real close to spot it from the alley. This was an all-white neighborhood, but no one was out on the streets at that hour. It was almost dark, and besides, we were in an unmarked vehicle, so we didn't attract any attention.

We got out of our vehicle and walked through the wooded area until we got close enough to readily identify the vehicle as belonging to the Goodyear store. There was no one around the truck, and we surmised that the thieves were waiting until dark to unload the stolen goods, either into the house or into some other vehicle that would come to the scene. We notified the dispatcher of what we had, and that we were going to back off and keep the place under surveillance. We then realized that if we both backed off, we would not be able to see the location and know when the thieves made their move. I decided that I would climb one of the many nearby trees located a short distance from the back yard. That way I could keep the scene under surveillance and have ample cover so I would not be spotted by the burglars. I informed the dispatcher of my intention; I can still hear her laughing.

She instructed Boswell to back off to a safe distance. She also instructed two other units to stand by within striking distance and to rush to my location upon my command. After climbing the tree and taking a seat on a limb about twenty feet off the ground, I turned my radio on real low (we all had walkie talkies at that time). What I didn't realize was that dogs could hear almost inaudible sounds. Several of the neighborhood dogs came to where I was and congregated under the tree and remained there whining.

I informed the dispatcher of this fact and informed her that I was going to turn my radio off until something happened. After waiting for more than an hour, it was well after dark. I saw a vehicle, a stake bed truck covered with a tarp, come up the alley and drive past the house and into the back yard, where it turned around and backed up until it was beside the stolen van. Two white males got out of the truck, and the back door of the house opened and a white male came outside and met with the other two subjects. They all went to the stolen van, opened the rear doors, and began taking items out of the vehicle. This was my cue to call for backup, which I did.

When I turned my radio on, the dogs, which had never left the vicinity of the tree, began whining again. I didn't care; I had to make my move. I could see myself fighting off a pack of dogs while trying to make my way to the suspects' location. When I could see the other officers approaching the suspects from several directions, I slid down the tree with the dogs barking and surrounding me, and headed to the scene in a blocking position to prevent their escape by vehicle. It was a good thing that the dogs were not vicious, just curious because of the noise from the police radio. Because of the element of surprise, we were able to apprehend all of the suspects without incident and the proper charges were lodged against them. All items stolen were recovered and returned to the store.

I recall an incident that happened while Boswell and I were assigned to the Collegeville area. We responded to a call with one shot. When we arrived on the scene we found a large crowd surrounding an apartment unit in the housing complex. We made our way inside and found the victim to be a young black male, around 17-18 years of age. It appeared that he had been shot in the chest area with a small caliber weapon. Upon examination, we found little if any blood around the entrance wound, with no exit wound. We realized that the victim was bleeding internally, which could be dangerous if medical help was not immediately available. We called for an ambulance and paramedics. The victim was conscious and coherent. He was able to give us the identity of the perpetrator and the circumstances of the shooting.

He had been shot some distance away but was able to walk home and collapsed on the living room floor, where we found him. After about twenty minutes and no ambulance, I called and inquired as to its status. I was told by the dispatcher that the medical help was blocked by a train on 29th Ave. and also on 35th Ave. and Huntsville Road. In other words, all access into Collegeville was blocked at the same time. Time passed and we had been on the scene over fifty minutes. I was standing by the victim and kept reassuring him that help would be there soon. He reached out and grabbed my pants leg and was holding on. After an hour had passed, he said, "I think I am going to die." I told him help would be there soon and he would be all right.

Pretty soon he stopped talking, but was still holding on to my pants leg. After an hour and five minutes, one train moved and the ambulance made it to the scene. They worked on the victim and took him away. I had to pry his hand away from my pants leg before he could be taken away from the scene. He was D.O.A., dead on arrival, at the hospital. I felt that if the trains were not blocking the entrance to the area and medical personnel could have gotten to the victim shortly after I called the incident in, the victim's life possibly could have been saved. He was alert and talking real strong for over forty minutes before fading. Two trains were still blocking tracks around the area. We were instructed by the dispatcher to give the conductor a citation for blocking a street for over twenty minutes without the train moving.

We parked our vehicle and walked up the tracks to the locomotives and cited the conductor for blocking a city street for an excessive amount of time without the train being in motion. From that day forward, if a train sat on the tracks without moving for twenty minutes, we would walk up the tracks to the locomotive and cite the conductor. At that time conductors rode in the locomotive with the engineer if the train did not have a caboose at the end of the line of box cars. The conductor was in charge of the train. I don't believe conductors ride on freight trains anymore. The word got around, and if a train was stopped and was not switching cars, all we had to do to get it moving was to drive up to the box cars that had the street blocked and turn on our emergency lights and siren, and the train would begin moving either backwards or forward until the blocked street was clear, and cars could proceed in and out of Collegeville. Pedestrians could get to their homes without having to crawl between boxcars, which was extremely dangerous for adults and children. Oh yes, we arrested the suspect in the shooting incident and charged him with homicide.

I feel until this day that it would have been something less than homicide if the streets hadn't been blocked by the trains, and medical help could have arrived shortly after they were dispatched. The situation in Collegeville has not changed greatly since that time. Trains still block the main arteries leading into and out of the area. The powers that be have talked about building overpasses over the railroad tracks, but to this day nothing has been done to alleviate the traffic problem for over forty years.

THE POLICE ACADEMY

About seven months after I was hired, I was assigned for training at the Police Academy. I had worked all this time in various capacities in the department with no formal training at all. I had been given a badge, uniforms, gun, and night stick and put to work. Their rationale was that there were not enough newly hired recruits to start a rookie class, and I had to be utilized until such time as there were ample recruits to start a training class. When classes finally started, there were two other black officers on board. They were Johnnie Johnson Jr., the second black officer hired, and Robert H. Boswell, the third black officer hired. Seven white officers rounded out the class, ten recruits in all. The first day was very interesting; some of the whites were friendly, some were not. We blacks excelled in physical training. Boswell was first in firearms, and I was second in academics in the final grades of the academy.

Johnnie got in trouble with the physical training instructor because he showed the instructor up in takedowns and come along techniques. Instead of giving in after awhile as the instructor wanted the students to do, Johnnie persisted and took the instructor down.

He made the instructor look bad in front of the white students and the instructor never forgot it, and he picked on Johnnie every chance he got. I got into it with one white recruit because I would always win during wrestling and takedown practices. He quit pairing off with me, and the instructor would not insist that he participate with me. It came to a head when we were all in a circle tossing the heavy medicine ball at each other's abdomen. You were supposed to let the ball hit your stomach, then grab the ball, not catch the ball before it hit you. I noticed that whenever I would toss the ball at him, he would catch the ball before it touched his abdomen. I fooled him the next time I got the ball. I faked a throw at him and his hands flew up to catch the ball. I didn't release the ball at that time. When his hands relaxed, I shot the ball into his stomach as hard as I could release it. It hit him square in his unprotected stomach, knocking him backwards to the ground.

He jumped up and rushed into me. I used his force to take him down with a judo throw. I also gave him a judo chop to the throat. By this time the instructor and some students pulled us apart. I had no more problems out of this recruit from then on. He failed to realize that I was an ex-paratrooper and was well versed in judo and jiu jitsu techniques. He had to find out the hard way. One day while we were in the classroom, three individuals dressed in Ku Klux Klan robes and hoods burst into the room, firing guns in the air. We found out later that they were firing blanks, and they were yelling, "Get those niggers," "Run, nigger, run." Afterward, all the whites were laughing, with the instructor saying it was just a joke. It was not funny at all to us black recruits. We knew that there were Klansmen in the department, but we didn't realize they would go to those extremes.

One evening as we were walking down the long hallway leaving the building, one recruit who was in the rear fired his weapon, either accidently or on purpose. The bullet passed by all of us and lodged in the exit door frame. The bullet hole is there to this day as a reminder to how tragic this could have been. If someone had been walking two abreast, one of the two could have been struck by the bullet. Prior to that incident, recruits wore their service weapons to and from the Academy. After this incident, recruits were forbidden to carry firearms in and around the Academy building, only on the firing range.

One day while in the classroom, representatives from the F.O.P., Fraternal Order of Police, visited the class. During the break, all of the white recruits were called into another room, where they talked to the F.O.P. representative. The black recruits were not invited. When the white recruits came back into the classroom, we asked them what was that all about. Some didn't say anything. A few told us that they were being recruited for membership in the F.O.P. They showed us the application sheets they had been given to fill out and return to the F.O.P. We were not recruited by the F.O.P. at that time, nor was I ever personally invited to join that organization. In later years, when there were some 12-plus blacks on the force, we organized our own fraternal organization, the "Birmingham Guardians," to represent blacks' interests as it related to the department. Much later, prior to my retirement, blacks were recruited and many did join the F.O.P. The original members were never asked to join as far as I know; I know that I was not. I couldn't care less, because whatever benefits were derived from the bargaining by the F.O.P., I, too, was a recipient of those benefits without having to pay dues to the organization.

The Birmingham Guardians played an important role in bargaining for the rights of blacks in the department and continued to be viable until such time as there was an influx of blacks joining the F.O.P., when it was finally disbanded. While in the Police Academy, we would attend classes four days and work the streets one night per week. Oftentimes we blacks would be used in undercover work during our Academy training. After Academy training, I had only about a couple of months until my probation period was up. All new recruits were on probation for one year, during which time they could be terminated without recourse. I felt much better when those couple of months were over; I could breathe a sigh of relief. The department had no field training officer program (F.T.O.). After graduation from the Academy, all recruits were placed on utility, which meant that they would be placed with senior officers on various shifts for a while for further on-the-job training. Some of us were placed on 11 p.m. to 7 a.m. on three wheelers.

COMMUNITY RELATIONS/POLICE ATHLETIC TEAMS

I was assigned to the Police Community Relations division under Captain G. Evans. My supervisor was Sergeant B. Hayes. Our job was to establish rapport with and foster good relations between the Police Department and the community. This wasn't an easy task, given the police record on human rights and police brutality in the past and present. It was our job to sell the idea that the department was in a mode of change and that our goal was fair treatment for every citizen, not just whites. The program sounded good, but what made it hard to sell was there were a lot of hard core officers who continued to mistreat and brutalize arrested black suspects. They called our unit "Nigger Lovers and Do-GOODERS."

What helped our cause was the fact that the department started in-service training for everyone on community relations. We continued to speak to community groups and visit schools and talk to children. Our unit decided to expand and include children in sports programs that would target primarily black children from low-income communities across the city. The program was named the Police Athletic Program (P.A.T.). It was patterned after the athletic program in New York and other big cities (PAL). Our program began very modestly with only two sports: baseball and basketball. Today, P.A.T. encompasses a multiplicity of sports. It was under the direction of Lieutenant R. (Bob) Boswell before his retirement and even included soccer and golf. We organized teams from as many communities as we could and recruited individuals as coaches that lived in the community and had knowledge of the kids.

Our primary sport was boys baseball. Birmingham became known nationwide for its boys baseball. We recruited police officers to act as coordinators of each team. The coordinators worked with the coaches and acted as a conduit between the teams and the P.A.T. staff. The baseball program was primarily during the summer and did not conflict with any programs the schools had going. There would be a playoff at the end of the session, and the winning team, its coach and all of the coordinators would get an expense-paid trip to a major league baseball city of choice. The team would play a Little League team from that city and visit a major league game played by the major league team of that city. The first city the winning team visited was New York. They won their game against a Little P.A.L. League team of all-stars and saw a New York Yankees game. Our basketball program did not achieve the fame of the baseball program initially, but in later years it became even more famous under the leadership of Lt. Boswell. I really enjoyed working in this program, because I felt that I was really making a difference.

BOSWELL'S HALL OF FAME INDUCTION: FAIRFIELD INDUSTRIAL HIGH SCHOOL

While working together in Collegeville, I accompanied Boswell to Fairfield Industrial High School, an all-black high school. Professor E.J. Oliver was principal and had been in that capacity for a long, long time. He had a reputation of being a strict disciplinarian. The majority of his former students all went on to achieve success in various fields of endeavor.

Officer Boswell was a former student of the school under the leadership of Professor Oliver. There was a hallway in the school that Professor Oliver had designated as the hall of fame. In this hallway were photos of and printed articles about all of the former students who had gone on to achieve success in life in some career field. He had designated a day for Boswell to be inducted into the school's hall of fame. Boswell had received the invitation, and because we were assigned to the same car, I accompanied him to the school to witness the occasion. After the induction ceremony, we were in Professor Oliver's office discussing policing with him and the many dangers associated with it. The professor asked Boswell how many individuals had he been forced to shoot in carrying out his duties as an officer. Boswell replied without hesitation, "Oh, I've shot seven men." Professor Oliver looked a little surprised but didn't make any comment to Boswell about his reply. I felt that he knew that Boswell was stretching the truth and embellishing what really had transpired.

He just said, "Hmmm." Then he asked me, "Officer Stover, how many men have you shot? I know how dangerous it is out there today." I said, "Professor, I have not had to shoot anybody." The professor replied, "You two worked together and have been for a couple of years. How is it that he shot all those men and you didn't have to shoot anyone?" I told him, "Well, Professor, I must have been off on the days that he had to shoot all those people." The only thing Professor Oliver said after that was, "Oh, I see."

I WAS CALLED INTO CHIEF'S OFFICE BECAUSE BOSWELL WAS BUSTED IN A NIGHTCLUB THAT DIDN'T HAVE PROPER LICENSES

I was at home on a Sunday minding my own business when I got a call from headquarters for me to report to the Chief's office on Monday at 8 a.m. I asked the officer if he knew what it was all about and he said that all he knew was that the Sheriff's Vice Squad had raided a night club called the 401 and Officer Boswell was caught up in the sting. This all-black club did not have all the necessary licenses for conducting business as a night club. I called Boswell to find out what happened. He told me that he was at the club and the Sheriff's detail did bust the place. They were preparing to take everyone to jail, but when they got to him and found out that he was a police officer, they didn't arrest anyone. This is what he told me. He said that the Sheriff reported his presence there to the Birmingham Police Department, because as Boswell put it, he caused the Sheriff Department to lose a lot of money they could have made on the arrests. Boswell stated that he told the Birmingham investigators that I had told him to meet me at the club on that night, for I had a singing protégé named Little R. Hatcher that I was to bring to the club for a tryout with the club's band. He told the investigators that the only reason he was there was the fact that I had told him to meet me there.

I knew this little R. Hatcher, but I had never told Boswell I would bring him to the 401 Club or for him to meet me there. I had no idea he was going to that night club. He told the police that the only reason he was present on that night was to meet me. Therefore, I was also requested to be in the Chief's office on that Monday morning. We arrived at the Chief's office on time and took a seat in the outer office. Officer McDavid was the receptionist, or desk officer. The outer office was crowded with white businessmen waiting to see the Chief. This was in the 1960s, and the word "nigger" was used frequently. Some whites used the word "nigra" instead of "nigger"; our Police Chief J. Moore was one of those. He meant well and was a decent man, but he was from the old school.

The Chief called out from the inner office to McDavid and said in a loud voice, "Are those two nigras out there yet?" McDavid answered and said, "Yes, Chief. Leroy and Robert are here." The Chief yelled back, "Ask them if they have their badges with them!" McDavid asked us, "Do you have your badges with you?" We told him that we did. He yelled back to the Chief, "Yes, Sir, they have their badges with them." The Chief yelled back to McDavid, "Good, then I can take them!" "Tell them two nigras to get on in here." McDavid told us, "Leroy and Robert, you can go in. The Chief will see you now." We both went into the inner office where the Chief and Deputy Chief J. Warren were seated. The Chief said, "You got your badges, don't you?" We said, "Yes, sir." He said, "I'll get them later. What is this about you being out there at that 409 Club?" I said, "It's the 401 club." I said I was never there, and I didn't tell Boswell to meet me there. The Chief said, "Robert, I think I'll take your badge for being at that club. In fact, I think I'll take both of your badges." Deputy Chief Warren spoke up and said, "Chief, quit playing with these men and get serious. Do what you are going to do or let them go."

Boswell spoke up and said that he didn't know the club didn't have the proper license. Chief Moore said, "I tell you what: if I ever hear of you two being out at that 403 club again, I will take your badges." I said, "401 club, Chief." He said, "Well, whatever it is, you better stay out of it. You can keep your badges. Get on back out there and keep those nigras straight in Collegeville. I hear y'all doing a good job out there." We left the office with great relief. For as long as he was Chief, every time Chief Moore saw Boswell and me, he would always ask, "You haven't been back to that 408, have you?" I would always say, "No sir. Chief, you know that you told us not to, and it is not the 408, it is the 4-0-1 Club."

MY PATROL EXPERIENCE WORKING WITH WHITE OFFICERS

I was assigned to Utility on the evening shift, which meant that I worked a number of different units with different officers. Some of the officers were nice and helpful; some were not. One thing they had in common, the senior man was in charge of the vehicle. The rookie didn't do anything without the senior officer's permission. It didn't matter whether the rookie was black or white. Unless it was an emergency situation when both officers responded, you were told when to get out of the car or when to sit tight. You were told when to drive, but you were allowed to write down information pertaining to calls from the dispatcher, and some even allowed me to answer the radio if I was driving.

Each officer had his own way of getting the job done. I learned something from each one, retaining that which I felt was good and beneficial to me as a professional and discarding the rest. Most of the officers I worked with would boast about how they had several cars and a cabin and boat on the lake. I wondered at the time how a patrolman could afford such luxury, and I found out later on. They would stop by certain residences on their beat, and while I sat in the car, they would bring a certain individual from the residence, be it man or woman, for them to meet the new black policeman. The officer called them "friends" of his. I learned much later that these were shot house operators and they were brought out so they could recognize me in case Vice used me in an undercover capacity to bust their operation. This way they recognized me and I would not be able to make a buy (purchase illegal whiskey). I learned later that these shot house owners paid certain police on a weekly basis in order that they could operate without fear of being busted.

Certain officers made good money during those times, probably more than they received from the city. I later learned that there were several well-known operators, such as R.K., J. M., M. R., and hundreds of others who plied their illegal trade with impunity under the watchful eye and protection of the local police. Several years later, as an internal affairs detective, I was instrumental in bringing several corrupt officers up on charges for taking bribes from shot house operators. I was able to get some operators to use marked money in making payments and come forth and testify against said officers. Some of these operators wanted out but were afraid of retaliation. When they were convinced that we in internal affairs were serious about breaking up this type of corruption, they cooperated with us, enabling our unit to bring several involved officers up on bribery charges.

After finishing the Police Academy, the second black officer and I were assigned to morning shift, 11 p.m. to 7 a.m., patrolling a beat in the downtown area on a three-wheel Harley Davidson motorcycle. There was a marked difference between this shift and the 3 p.m. to 11 p.m. shift. There were no so-called "Senior Car Men." Everyone on this shift was young and inexperienced, with no one having much over three to four years. They were a much more friendly bunch, with all of us being in the same boat, so to speak. Our primary duty was to prevent burglaries and break-ins on our beats. Our district was mostly businesses, with a sprinkling of residences in the area from about 12th Street to about 26th Street on the north side of the city, and from about 12th Street to about 32nd Street on the south side of town.

The width of this patrol area extended from 8th Avenue North to about 8th Avenue South. My three-wheeler beat was from 12th Street to 20th Street and from 8th Avenue to 3rd Avenue North. On this beat during this time there were a few residences on the western and northern end of my beat. During the hours of my shift, I encountered everything from derelicts and winos on the lower end of the beat to pimps, hustlers and ladies of the evening in the 4th and 5th Avenue downtown area. I also had to deal with traffic violations, as well as present a highly visible presence to deter robbers, pickpockets, flim-flam artists and other petty criminals who preyed on the crowds that frequented the area at night.

My beat was very busy until the wee hours of the morning, after all of the bars had closed and the crowd had thinned out. I then concentrated on checking the front and rear of businesses for possible break-ins. In order to effectively check the front of the businesses, I would ride on the sidewalks in front of the businesses, and ride down the alleys in order to check the rear. While riding the alleys, I would turn the head light off and use a plug-in spotlight or my flashlight. That way I was able to surprise several burglars who had broken into businesses and were still inside. I would call for back up and make the arrests. I thank God that back in the day, burglars were not usually armed; not so in today's world.

Yes, we stopped speeders and those who ran red lights on our three-wheelers or pop cycle wagon. Most people didn't know it, but we could do in excess of 65 to 70 miles per hour (mph) on those Harleys; a lot of violators found out the hard way. I was patrolling in the area near 5th Avenue and 17th Street North one night when I heard gunshots in the vicinity of 4th Avenue, near the pool hall in the Masonic Temple building. I notified the dispatcher and proceeded to the location. Upon arrival, I observed a crowd standing over an individual who was lying on the sidewalk. The crowd yelled to me, "He's been shot, and there goes the man that did it!" They pointed to an individual who was walking west on 4th Avenue from that location. I took off after him on my Harley, while notifying the dispatcher of the situation and to send an ambulance to the scene. When the suspect heard me behind him, he looked back and took off running. I easily gained on him and got opposite him when he left the sidewalk and ran across an open grassy area toward the A.G. Gaston Funeral Home building. One P. Williams, a part-time employee of the funeral home and part-time radio disc jockey, was standing outside looking in our direction, when he saw us headed in his direction more than a block away. I stopped my Harley, got off, and began chasing the suspect on foot. I yelled "Police, halt!"

The suspect turned, and when he did he stumbled, dropping his gun. He didn't have time to pick it up, so he kept running toward the front of the funeral home. I stopped to pick up the gun and I temporarily lost sight of him as he turned the corner of the building. He was only about 20 feet ahead of me and I knew that I could catch him if he continued on 15th Street. P. Williams was standing in front of the business at that time and I heard him yell, "Don't come in here!" When I rounded the corner, P.W. was standing in front of the doorway, pointing to the inside of the funeral home. P.W. told me, "I tried to stop him, but he pushed me aside and went on in." P.W. and I checked the front of the building, but he wasn't there. P.W. said that he was still inside the building, for the rear door was locked. We checked every room in the building except the morgue. We concluded that he had to be hiding in there. We entered the morgue, which was semi-dark. P.W. turned on some more light so we could see better. There were several bodies laid out on either side of the aisle. All the bodies were laid on their backs, covered with their feet pointing up.

As we walked past the bodies, I noticed that one body was not barefoot, but had on shoes under the sheet. Upon looking closer, I noticed that the sheet was moving, where he was breathing in and out. I touched P.W. and showed it to him and motioned for him to be quiet. I said aloud, "Well, P.W., I guess he got out some kind of way, for he's not in here. Let's go." As we started back up the aisle, I took my night stick and gave the suspect a hard blow across the shins. He jumped up yelling. I said, "Well, what do we have here? One that has risen from the dead!" While he was still whining about his legs hurting, P.W. and I rolled him over and I handcuffed him with his hands behind his back. I escorted him outside of the funeral home to wait for backup. When the backup arrived, the suspect was then taken to the scene, where he was positively identified as the shooter. I discovered that the shooting was the result of a pool gambling debt. The suspect was properly charged and taken to jail.

Another night I was in the 700 block of 15th Street when I came upon two females of color engaged in a fight. They were going after each other like cats and dogs. I notified the dispatcher, jumped off my Harley, and proceeded to break up the fight. As I approached the two females, one pulled the other's wig off her head. The fight got even more ferocious. I grabbed both females and tried to pull them apart, to no avail. They knew that I was the police, but that didn't seem to matter. I backed off for a moment to decide what to do next. They were on the ground by this time.

I waded into the fray, grabbed one of the females and was able to separate her from her assailant. As I was holding this one female, the other one got up and came towards us, trying to get to the one I had. I was trying to handcuff the one I had and at the same time ward off the other one. I got the one I had cuffed, all the while holding the other one off with my back. She reached across my shoulder and grabbed my necktie and began pulling it, choking me. We wore those long neckties that you tied around your neck (the department later came out with clip-on ties). To get out of my predicament, I turned and hit her as hard as I could in her stomach with my fist. She doubled over and I let her have a right to the jaw. She hit the ground like a sack of potatoes, out for the moment. She wasn't going anywhere and I had only one set of cuffs, so I handcuffed the one I had in physical custody to the back of the Harley and requested a transport vehicle. I pulled the other assailant over to the Harley and sat her down, propped up against the three-wheeler, where I could keep an eye on both of them. She was still in that position when backup arrived. They were both taken to jail. I explained to my sergeant as to what had transpired. He stated that I did what was necessary to overcome their physical resistance and affect the arrest.

I recall another incident that happened one night as I was headed south on 17th Street around 3 o'clock in the morning. As I crossed 5th Avenue, I saw a car headed east, stopped at the light. I continued south on 17th Street and turned west on 3rd Ave., which was not a one-way street during that time. When I reached 15th Street, I headed north. When I reached 5th Avenue, I looked and saw a car stopped at the light at 17th Street. From two blocks away it looked like the same car that I had seen at the light earlier. I turned east on 5th Avenue and realized that it was the same car. The driver, a middle age black man, was fast asleep behind the wheel. It's no telling how long he had been sitting there asleep before I drove by the first time. I kept tapping on the car's window until he woke up. I asked him to wind his window down, which he did. I smelled alcohol, so I asked him had he been drinking, and he said that he had had a few beers earlier. I asked him to step out of the car and had him go through a few exercises and he did pretty well on those. He said that he was just trying to get home.

I didn't feel too comfortable with letting him drive off in the car, but he didn't appear to be drunk and I hadn't really witnessed him driving, so I decided to give him a break. I could have arrested him for possession of a vehicle while under the influence. So, I told him to walk over to the parking lot behind Willie May's Place, a bar on the corner of 17th Street and 5th Avenue North, and I would drive his car over there. I parked his car, told him that I was giving him a break, and for him to get in the back seat and take a nap, for he was not in any shape to continue driving right then. He got in the back of the car and I told him that he would be safe, for I would come by often and check on him. He said thank you and I left to continue my rounds. I drove by a couple of times within an hour and a half, and the car was still parked on the lot. However, some two and a half hours later, the unit that patrols from 20th Street to 26th Street called me and asked me to meet him at the Redmont Hotel, located at 20th Street and 5th Ave. North. When I arrived, I saw the officer standing beside the same car that had been parked on the parking lot on 17th Street. The same person I had left on the back seat to sleep it off was again behind the wheel. To compound matters worse, he had jumped the curb and hit a light pole, which stopped the car. Neither the pole nor the car sustained any visible damage. A witness stated that the car had just left the light at 20th Street and, proceeding slowly, veered to the right, striking the curb and the light pole some 20 feet past the intersection.

The officer told me that the driver told him that a police officer down the street had talked to him and told him that he could drive on. I got the driver out of his car, confronted him, and he told the officer the truth, about how I had given him a break, told him not to drive, but to get in the back seat and sleep it off, and that after a while he took it on his own to try and get home, for he was overdue at home. The officer asked me what I wanted to do I said, "What I should have done before was to put him in jail. I can prove that he drove his car from 17th Street to 20th Street, and that he was under the influence of alcohol. And that he caused an accident." He was charged, arrested and his car towed. I realized then that you just can't do some people a favor; it can backfire on you.

THE ARREST OF THE PARKING METER BURGLAR

One night as I was patrolling my beat on my Harley three-wheeler, a call went out from the officer on the adjacent beat stating that he had come upon a parking meter burglar in the 1600 block of 2nd Ave. North and he requested assistance. I, along with several other three-wheel units, responded to the location given. Several units were on the scene when I arrived. I observed a young black male suspect in his early twenties lying on the ground, with several white officers standing over him. The suspect had on a long overcoat, the pockets of which were filled with assorted coins, as well as his trouser pockets.

A large screwdriver was lying on the ground nearby. The parking meters were constructed of a type metal that made them easy to break into (vandalize). All one would need was a large screwdriver to pop them open. As a result, vandalism was a common occurrence in the area where parking meters were utilized, particularly during the hours of darkness in areas on streets that were not well lighted and there was little or no vehicular traffic during the night time. There was evidence that this suspect had plied his trade for some time and for a great distance on 2nd Avenue, before he was spotted and apprehended by the officer whose beat he was operating on. One could observe busted parking meters for several blocks on both sides of 2nd Avenue North. The officer whose beat the burglaries occurred on was yelling at the suspect, "I'll teach you to break in meters on my beat and try to run from me."

The suspect was so heavy laden with coins that he couldn't run, even if he had tried to. This officer began beating the suspect with his night stick, and the other four or five officers present took out their night sticks and joined in the fray. The suspect began squirming, twisting and kicking, trying to avoid the blows. The suspect had not been handcuffed prior to his being beaten. A sergeant drove up while the suspect was being beaten by about five white officers. I was standing nearby. The sergeant told me to get in there and help those officers beat that "black thieving bastard's ass." I proceeded to obey the sergeant's orders. I stepped in and grabbed one of the suspect's legs, while trying to avoid all those flailing night sticks. I was hit on the shoulder by a night stick and I turned the leg loose and told the sergeant, "I ain't going back in that crowd, because somebody hit me." The sergeant laughed and said, "Well, Leroy, it's dark out here. You forgot to smile so your teeth could show and they (the white officers) could see where you were." I told him it was not funny to me. The sergeant then ordered the officers to stop beating the suspect. He was handcuffed and charged with burglary, theft and, of course, resisting arrest. Some of the officers told me, "We're sorry, Leroy, but we didn't see you." My problem was there was no reason to beat the suspect in the first place, and the sergeant's remarks were totally racist in nature. I was so disgusted, but there wasn't anything I could do but get on my Harley and go back to my assigned beat.

MY COLLISION WITH JOHNNIE JOHNSON JR'S THREE-WHEELER

One night while patrolling downtown, my three-wheeler ran low on gas. I contacted Johnnie and he indicated that his vehicle was low on gas also.

We decided to go and refill our vehicles at the city's maintenance complex on Sixth Ave. South. We left downtown and headed west on First Ave. North, where we would turn south on the street that crosses the railroad tracks and continues past the then-Sears warehouse. This was a shortcut that all three-wheelers used to get to the gas pumps on Six Ave. South. I believe that the street is Fourth Place. As Johnnie and I approached that street on First Ave., Johnnie made a traffic light. I was about twenty-five yards behind and had to stop for the red light. From the distance, I could see his vehicle make a left turn and head south toward the set of railroad tracks about one and a half blocks from where his vehicle made the left turn from First Ave. North. Unknown to me, a train was stopped, blocking the street. Johnnie had stopped his three-wheeler, turned off his engine and lights, and was waiting for the train to move. There were no street lights in that area and it was hard to see a stopped train, or a stopped vehicle with no lights on.

When the light changed in my favor, I sped west on First Ave. and turned south on what I believed was Fourth Place. Johnnie's vehicle was nowhere in sight. In the darkness, I failed to see the dark train box cars or Johnnie's stopped vehicle. I had traveled about one block before I realized that a train and Johnnie were stopped directly in front of me. I applied the brakes, but I couldn't stop in time to avoid hitting Johnnie's vehicle square in the rear. Our vehicles didn't have seat belts, and I was thrown over my windshield onto the back of Johnnie's three-wheeler. I landed on the flat area of his vehicle and was only slightly shaken up. The bumper on Johnnie's vehicle was only slightly damaged, and my vehicle had bounced backwards after the front tire had struck the other vehicle's bumper. Needless to say, the vehicles were made out of much better material that they are today. Johnnie, being where he was, prevented me from going underneath those stopped boxcars and undoubtedly prevented much more serious injury to my vehicle and myself. We talked and laughed about it later, but it could have been much worse. After that incident, our sergeant forbade more than one three-wheeler officer to go for gas at a time.

THE STANDOFF AT QUEEN'S LOUNGE: "THE LONGEST EIGHT MINUTES"

On this particular night I was working an extra job at Queen's, or People's Lounge, located at the 4100 block of Airport Highway. I was assigned to work from about 11 p.m. to about 4 a.m., or until everyone left the premises. The place was almost full of people when I arrived. When working an off-duty job, police regulations dictate that the officer must call in to police communications information concerning the officer's identity, employee number, the name and location of the business and the hours to be spent on the job. When all of this information is given to police communications, the officer is covered on his extra job in the same manner as when he is on his regular job with the city. He also has direct access to police assistance in case of trouble. This is expedited because his location is already known.

On this particular night, after arriving at the club, I went to the kitchen area behind the bar to use the telephone to call headquarters as directed. Unknown to me, a group of thugs were already in the club. As I was leaving the kitchen and approaching the bar area, several black male members of another group had entered the club and pulled guns on the group that was already in the club. Naturally, this group pulled out their guns also. What confronted me were two groups with weapons drawn, facing each other from across the large lounge. Customers were crouched down, afraid to move because shooting could start at any moment.

As soon as I was aware of the situation, I told the owner to call the police and tell them that I needed help now. The owner was placing the call as I walked out to the lounge area. With my gun holstered, I walked out in front of the bar and talked to the two groups. Nobody pointed a gun at me, nor did anyone start shooting. They were yelling back and forth at each other, and I felt that the least incident could set off a shooting spree. I told them, "May I have your attention." When they quieted down and looked in my direction, I took a couple of steps forward. I told them, "I would like for you to put your guns away. I can't make you, for it is only one of me." Nobody put their guns up. I went on: "This is a nice lounge run by decent people. You have all been customers here at one time or another and everything was cool. I don't think you want to shoot up the place and possibly get killed or hurt and kill or hurt innocent people. You know most of these people here, they know you, and you know the owner and the owner knows you." I had been talking for over five minutes and they were paying attention to me.

They could not see the front, for there were people standing near the door. I was hoping that back up arrived soon, but that they would not come bursting through the door, for that could set off a shooting spree. It was obvious that neither side wanted to back down, but nobody fired a first shot, so I felt that nobody really wanted to be the first to shoot. I got bolder and said, "Why don't you guys just call it a draw? You have proved your point. I know that you are not afraid of each other or me. What you need to do is stand down, put your guns away, go outside, put them up and come back and have fun. I see that you don't want to hurt anybody."

At this time several white police officers had quietly entered the front door, unseen by the young men. When there were about ten officers inside the club along the wall, I said, Come on, let's go outside and put your guns away." They all turned around and were confronted by police officers with guns drawn. The sergeant in charge yelled, "Police! Drop your guns, we have you covered!" They all dropped their guns and were placed under arrest. There were no injuries and 13 guns were recovered. It seemed as if I was talking forever waiting for backup to arrive, but I was told that it was only eight minutes. That was the longest eight minutes I had ever experienced. The management and the customers were grateful that the situation was handled without bloodshed. I thanked God that it worked out as it did.

THE ARREST OF TWO ROWDY DRUNKS BY 3/5 OF A MAN

I was working with a white officer and we were patrolling in the downtown area when we observed two white males who appeared to be intoxicated, staggering up 5th Ave., headed in the direction of the terminal train station. We stopped our car, got out and approached the two subjects, who had stopped when they saw the police car and tried to straighten up and appear sober, hoping that we would pass them by. When we reached the two suspects, we found that they both smelled strongly of alcohol. Their eyes were bloodshot and their speech was slurred. They were classic examples of drunken individuals. They both failed the sobriety tests given, including dexterity: putting finger to nose and walking a straight line. They both admitted to drinking most of the evening at different bars, and one of them had about a half-empty bottle of whiskey on his person.

At that time a person could be arrested for being in an intoxicated state on a city street, or having an open container of legal whiskey bought at a state store, or having a bottle of illegal "Moonshine" whiskey on his/her person. We explained to these individuals that they were under arrest for public intoxication, and we poured the whiskey out on the ground. My partner took one subject and placed him against the police car to frisk him. As I was placing the other subject on the car, he began to struggle and told me, "Nigger, you can't arrest me. I'm a white man and you are just 3/5 of a man. The government ruled that a long time ago and it has not changed."

I was familiar with what he was referring to, for back during Reconstruction the government allowed southern whites to count Negros as 3/5 of a person to bolster their voting power. I told the subject, "If I am just 3/5 of a person, what does that make you?" I subdued him and slammed him up against the car, frisked him and handcuffed him, before putting him in the back of the police car. I told him, "It's a shame, you being a 100% white man and fortified with alcohol, would allow a 3/5 of a person, a black man, degrade and humiliate you by arresting you in the presence of all these white people that have gathered around." He made the statement: "When I was in Mississippi, nigger police couldn't arrest white people. They would have to call for white policemen." I told him, "Aren't you glad that you are now in Birmingham, Alabama, where even, as you say, 3/5 of a person can arrest anyone that violates the law?" I told him, "Once you get out of jail, you can go back to Mississippi and warn your good old boy buddies to stay out of Birmingham, Alabama, for they got 3/5 of a person nigger police that can even arrest a white man."

HOMICIDE AT THE "TANGO PALACE"

On certain nights I would work off-duty security for a night club named the "Tango Palace," operated by "Big George" Nichols. This club was upstairs on the corner of Second Ave. and 22nd Street North. On one particular night as I was working, one Gaines Hicks came in the club with an entourage of five or six young ladies, all attractive and all well dressed. Gaines Hicks himself was a snappy dresser and was well known in the night club circuit. There were rumors as to his line of business, but all I knew of him was that he frequented night spots and that he was always accompanied by a bevy of young ladies. He was respectful and friendly towards me and we would often talk as he watched or engaged in shooting pool in the pool hall area of the night club.

On one particular night, Hicks came into the club with at least five attractive young ladies. Later, as I was near the pool hall area, I observed a man known to me as Indee Farris approach the table where Hicks and company were seated. This man became engaged in a heated conversation with one of the ladies at the table. The man grabbed the lady by the hand and tried to pull her up from her seat, but the lady wouldn't budge. Hicks said something to the man and then got up from the table and came over to where I was standing. Hicks explained to me that the man who had pulled on the lady was Indee Farris, estranged husband to the lady in question. According to Hicks, the two had been separated for many months, and the lady was back staying with her mother. According to Hicks, the lady was a friend of his lady companions. She had asked his companions if she could go to the club with them that night and they had agreed to take her along. Hicks stated that he and his companions had gone by the lady mother's house and picked her up. According to Hicks, this was the first time this lady had gone out with them. He stated that he was not familiar with her before that night. He stated that he told this to Indee Farris, and that since he had picked her up at her mother's house, he felt obligated to take her back there. He stated that he told Farris that he could go to her mother's house and talk to her after he had taken her home.

I told Hicks to go back to the table, and I called Farris over to the pool hall area, where I talked to him. He explained that they were, indeed, separated and living separately. She was at her mother's house. He stated that he didn't like the fact that Hicks had brought his estranged wife to the club and he was going to take her out of there. I asked him if she wanted to go with him and he said that she did not, that she wanted to go back to her mother's house.

I told him that under the circumstances it would be better if he let Hicks take the lady back to where he picked her up from, which was her mother's house. He could see and talk to her there, and if she wanted to come home with him, good, and if not, he could not force her to do so. I warned Farris that I would not tolerate any violence or disturbance of any kind by him toward his estranged wife while she was in the club. Farris told me that I was right and that he would not bother her or Hicks anymore, but would talk to her after Hicks had returned her to her mother's house.

After our conversation, Farris left the club by exiting down the stairway. Later that night, I saw Hicks and his entourage leave the club by way of the stairwell. I was standing near a window facing 22nd Street, where I could observe Hicks' car, which was parked on the east side of 22nd Street near the intersection of 2nd Ave. North. I was watching as Hicks and his company exited the door of the club and walked about thirty feet to where his car was parked at the curb. Hicks unlocked his car and opened the doors for the ladies. As Hicks came back around to the driver's side, a male who had been hiding beside a car parked on the opposite side of the street, jumped up and ran across the street to Hicks' car and jumped up on the trunk and began firing a hand gun downward at Hicks.

I recognized the shooter as Indee Farris, who I had talked to concerning his estranged wife, and who had left the club several hours earlier. Farris fired several rounds at Hicks, with several striking him in the head and upper part of his body. Hicks fell to the sidewalk, and the crowd that was leaving the club scattered in all directions, with many rushing back into the club, creating congestion on the stairway. As Hicks fell to the sidewalk, the shooter, Indee Farris, jumped off the car and started running back across 22nd Street. I didn't see where he went, for at this time I was heading toward the stairway to get to the street below. I had to literally push my way through the throng of people trying to get back inside the club.

There was total chaos, with people pushing and screaming. When I finally pushed my way to the sidewalk and reached the crime scene, I observed Gaines Hicks lying face up on the sidewalk beside his car. I checked his condition and was reasonably sure that he was deceased; I called for backup and paramedics. When the first patrol units arrived, I briefed them on what had occurred and instructed them to cordon off the crime scene and get the names of all possible witnesses, including the ladies that were with Hicks in the club, in order that they could be interviewed later by homicide detectives.

With everything under control and while waiting for the coroner to arrive, I walked across the street in the direction I had observed Farris run. I began walking south on the sidewalk of 22nd Street, when about thirty yards ahead of me I observed the figure of what appeared to be a man crouched behind a parked car and looking in the direction of the crime scene. When the subject realized that I was approaching his location, he jumped up and started running south on the sidewalk of 22nd Street North. When the subject started running, I recognized him as Indee Farris, the suspect in the shooting of Hicks, the same person that I had talked to in the club and the same person I had observed on top of Hicks' car trunk, firing a weapon directly at him. I yelled at Farris, "Stop! Police!" but he didn't slow up, but got faster.

I got on my walkie talkie and notified communications that I had the suspect in the homicide in sight and was chasing him on foot. I gave our location and direction of travel and requested assistance. The suspect crossed 1st Ave. North and headed toward Morris Ave. with me in hot pursuit. I yelled "Halt, Police! Stop or I'll shoot!" I was about 25 yards behind him at this point, but was gaining on him. I was not going to shoot him with him running and me running also. I was not that good of a shot to wing him in the leg or something; it would just be my luck to hit him in the back or the head. Policy did not prohibit my shooting at a suspect when he was a fleeing, felony suspect in a possible homicide.

Where 22nd Street crosses 1st Ave North, it becomes elevated and there is a driveway that runs beside 22nd Street and leads to Morris Ave. When Farris crossed 1st Ave. North, he headed down this driveway toward Morris Ave., with me in hot pursuit. South of Morris Ave., there were railroad tracks between Morris Ave. and 1st Ave. South. In this area there were tall grass and weeds, over head high, which could offer concealment for the suspect. Realizing this, I increased my speed and was gaining on him when he looked back and fired one round in my direction, but not directly at me. That may have been his last round, for he didn't fire anymore. He was firing a small semi-automatic weapon.

At this point we both were south of 1st Ave. and headed toward the tall Johnson grass near the railroad tracks. I stopped, pulled my weapon, and fired one round at the fleeing suspect. I fired low, hoping to strike him in the leg, but no such luck. He disappeared into the tall weeds. It was dark down there and I gave up the chase and waited on the backup units. We didn't enter the tall grass, but went around to 1st Ave. South and searched that side of the tracks.

There were tall weeds on either side of the tracks and the suspect could have gone east or west on the tracks without being detected. We gave up the hunt, and the next day Farris' lawyer turned him in to police headquarters, where he was formally charged with murder, thus ending the episode of the homicide at the Tango Palace.

WORKING AN EXTRA JOB AS SECURITY/THE CRIPS & BLOODS ENCOUNTER AT TEE'S PLACE

I worked an extra job as security at Tee's Place on Second Ave. North for over twenty years. I recall an incident that occurred one night as I was working that assignment: two gangs, the Crips and the Bloods, who had an ongoing feud between them, decided to meet up at Tee's and settle the issue. Around two a.m. I was inside the club, when the crowd that was on the outside and those that were exiting the building made a mad rush back inside the club. They were all yelling, "The Crips and Bloods are outside and they are going to have a shoot-out!" They were yelling, "The police need to go out there, for there will be a lot of killing out there, for they all have their guns out." I pushed my way through the crowd to the front door. I was working alone with no backup.

Before exiting the building, I told the owner I was going outside, and for him to call for backup. Upon exiting the building, I observed about fifty to sixty armed gang members, half wearing something red, which identified them as Bloods, and half wearing something blue, identifying them as Crips. They all were armed with semi-automatic or automatic weapons, including Uzis and AK47s. They were lined up on either side of Second Ave. North, each group facing the other in a standoff. I approached the groups and walked to the middle of Second Ave. North, directly between the two groups. I never cleared leather, but kept my weapon holstered. I knew them and they knew me. Those that were old enough were customers of Tee's Place at one time or another, but not as a group. They would leave their weapons in their cars, for they were aware that no weapons were allowed inside the club. All persons entering the club would have to pass through a metal detector and be screened for weapons.

As I walked out into the street, I kept thinking about what I was going to say to the gangs. There were people who had ventured outside the club after I came out and were standing back at a distance to see what I would do. I knew that backup was on the way and I knew that if and when the backup units arrived, that would trigger shooting on both sides. I knew that I would have to defuse the situation and get the gangs out of there before backup arrived. I knew that once backup arrived, all hell could break loose, especially with those trigger-happy young officers on the eleven p.m. to seven a.m. shift who hated and feared the gangs.

I told the gang members: "You all know me. I have always treated you fair! I didn't come out here to confront you with arms, for I am only one person with a nine millimeter and you have all kinds of weapons. As you can see, I knew it would be foolish for me to try and make you put down your weapons. I came out here to reason with you in order to save the lives of innocent people. If you have a shoot-out, a lot of innocent persons will be hurt. The club will also suffer a black mark on its record and no one here has ever done you any harm, and as patrons of this club you have been shown nothing but respect. I can't stop you from having your shoot-out if you can't settle your differences any other way, but I do ask you out of respect for me and the club owners that it not be settled here, where a lot of innocents will be harmed. I tell you what: if you must have a shoot-out there is Legion Field not far away that has large parking areas where you can shoot to your hearts' delight. That way you will not have harmed any innocent people, and those of you that are left will be able to visit the club as before, without your weapons of course."

When I finished my speech, there was silence for a moment. Then the leaders said, "Captain, you have a point; let's go, men." They all went to their various vehicles and drove off in the direction of Legion Field. As they drove off, the people who had ventured out of the club gave me a round of applause. The club owner came out and asked me how I got them to leave. I told him that I explained to the gangs that it was in the best interest of everyone involved that they take their feud somewhere else like Legion Field, where it would be less likely that they would harm innocent bystanders, and they agreed with me. We listened for a while but didn't hear any gunfire coming from the direction of Legion Field, so I figured that whatever grudges there was between the two groups were not worth being injured or dying for, and that they could co-exist peacefully. I don't think that they really wanted to have a shoot-out, but neither group wanted to back down, and my talk gave them a chance to back out gracefully and save face at the same time. No one was more relieved than I was as I got on my walkie-talkie and canceled the backup units, indicating that everything was 10-4 okay. In the coming weeks, some of the members from both gangs frequented the club, and many of them told me that they appreciated the fact that I didn't try to run them off or call backup officers on them, but allowed them to leave voluntarily. I told them that I was just glad that it ended peacefully.

TEE'S PLACE + UNEXPECTED + FACE-TO-FACE WITH AN ARMED SUSPECT

On one occasion as I was working my off-duty job at Tee's, I suddenly came face to face with an armed shooting suspect. On this particular night I was outside of the club, checking areas to prevent vehicular break-ins and thefts. On the nights that the club was open for business, patrons' cars would be parked for several blocks on either sides and in the rear of the club, all the way to First Ave. North. Periodically I would exit the club on an irregular basis and patrol these parking areas. On more than one occasion I was able to arrest several burglars and would-be car thieves in the act. On this occasion I was about a block away in the area of Rib-It-Up Barbecue checking vehicles, when I heard a shot that seemed to have come from near the front of the club. I started running in that direction and observed a crowd dispersing from the front of the club, scattering in all directions, with most of them headed in my direction. As I turned the corner in the rear of Rib-It-Up, I suddenly came face to face with a young man with a gun in his hand running directly toward me.

We were about five feet from each other and my gun was still in my holster. I recognized the young man as a regular patron who never was a problem for anyone and was always respectful to me. We both stopped running when we were about three feet apart, facing each other. He had his gun in his hand pointing at me; my gun was in my holster. He said, "Sarge" (a lot of them still called me "Sarge" from the time that I was a sergeant, even though I was now a Captain.) The young man said, "I'm just trying to get away. Four men jumped me while I was in line trying to get into the club, and I fired my weapon into the air to get away. I didn't shoot anybody. The only reason I brought my gun tonight was because they had threatened me all week because of a girl, and I knew that they would be looking for me to beat me up." He said, "I am trying to leave and go home and I would appreciate it if you would just let me go." He asked me to let him go and I didn't have my weapon out and he had his drawn.

I looked down toward the front of the club and didn't see anyone on the ground, so I figured that he was telling the truth. I said to him, "Go on, brother, go home and don't bring that gun to the club again." He said, "Thank you. Sarge," and continued running around Rib-It-Up toward First Ave. North. I continued running down the driveway toward the front of the club, where I met the owner, who was coming out of the club with his gun in his hand.

He told me that some guys jumped on a customer who was in line, and the customer fired a shot and got away in the crowd. He asked me, "Did you see anyone with a gun running in your direction?" I told him that when I heard the shot, I was over a block away checking vehicles, and that as I got within sight of the club, I saw people running in all directions, including toward me. I said, "You know, it's dark up there and it was hard to make out who had what, for everyone was running." I said, "I am glad that no one was hurt, but I think that after being jumped on by four men, he was probably just trying to get away." The owner said, "Yeah, I guess you're right. Anyway, he's gone now and nobody was hurt." I said, "I am sure that if he had wanted to, he could have shot those guys. He just wanted to get them off him and leave." The owner said, "I wish I knew who he was, so I could bar him from coming back to the club." I didn't see the young man for over a month.

Then one night he and his lady friend showed up and were standing outside. I went out and talked to him. He said that he had been afraid to come back to the club, because he thought that I had reported him to the owner. He stated that he had a permit for his gun and showed it to me, and stated that he kept it in the trunk of his car. I told him that he had told me the truth. I let him know that he had the drop on me and still asked my permission to let him go. I told him that he had never caused any problems and he was free to frequent the club as often as he wished. He thanked me for what I did for him and was a model patron from then on.

EPISODE OF PROMOTIONAL EXAM FOR RANK

After a couple of years with the department, I became aware that after three years of service one would be eligible to take the promotional examination for the rank of Sergeant, providing his monthly evaluation was 85 or over. To prevent one from taking the promotional exam, all a supervisor had to do was give him an evaluation of less than 85, even if all other criteria had been met. Routinely, if one had less than three years of service, one's evaluation would not be 85. Even the sharpest officer would not receive an 85 evaluation if he had less than three years, and therefore was not eligible in terms of years of service in the department to take a promotional examination.

However, if you were in the "in crowd," in good standing with the powers that be, and they felt that you needed a shot at the promotional examination, or someone in higher authority wanted to see you promoted once you reached three years with the department, your six months' evaluation would jump to an 85 or above, even though leading up to this particular grading period your evaluation was considerably lower. So, officers with leadership potential who aspired to advance to the rank of supervisor were at the mercy and whim of their immediate supervisors as to whether or not they would be graded high enough to take the examination when it became available.

This was the situation in which I and the other black officers eligible for promotion found ourselves. First, it was the rank and file white officers who tried to persuade us from taking a promotional exam by saying, "You don't want to be a Sergeant; you can make more money as a patrolman working extra jobs." Some didn't want to leave the streets because they were lucrative for them, because of monies they acquired from illegal operations. Some would even tell us that we could make more money at Acipco and U.S. Pipe, who were hiring workers regularly. Beside that, if we happened to be working under a racist supervisor, we couldn't hope for a favorable evaluation. We found that when we went to the police library to check out study books for the upcoming Sergeant's examination, we were told that they were all checked out. This was months before any examination. As the examination got closer, white officers were checking out study books with regularity. I finally ordered some promotional examination books by mail for every rank from Sergeant up to Captain. They were excellent books, full of relevant material. One thing in my favor was my transfer to Ensley (West) Precinct. This precinct was staffed by officers who did not sit well with the good old racist boys downtown.

They didn't condone all the brutality against blacks and corruption that went on downtown. Every officer that disagreed or spoke out concerning brutality or corruption downtown was shipped out to Ensley. The Ensley officers were known as outcasts. I, too, was transferred to Ensley after my run-in with the white officer concerning his disparity in the treatment of black and white traffic offenders and the black church incident, where he wanted to ticket black churchgoers on Sunday and I would not let it happen. At the Ensley Precinct, I was treated with dignity and respect. I was given all assistance possible to acclimate myself to the workings of that precinct. The white officers were aware that the police library would not allow blacks to check out promotional reading material, so they would check out the necessary books in their names, study them, and let me have them until they were due to be returned. I would make notes from all of the relevant books necessary for the Sergeant, Lieutenant, and Captain's examinations. My notes were so thorough, and with the reading material I ordered, I never had to check out books from the library, even when I was able to do so later on.

With the assistance from the guys at the West Precinct and a decent supervisor who gave me the rating I rightly deserved (an above 85 evaluation), I was eligible to take the Sergeant's examination. After four years on the force, I passed the Sergeant's examination in the top three overall and was subsequently promoted before my fifth year. During the early 1980s, the federal government and the City reached an agreement because of past discrimination in hiring and promotions, called a Consent Decree. I recall an agreement finalized in 1982, whereby if a minority was on a promotional list and there was only a certain number of promotion positions open in a department and the minority's name was farther down the list, then the department would have to pass over eligible whites to get to the minority individual so that his name would be within the number of promotion positions. So, if a minority, let's say, was number eighteen on the eligible list and there were only seven positions open for, let's say, Sergeant in the department, then the minority's name would leapfrog (skip) over white officers ahead of him on the eligible list until his name fell within the available slots, say at number seven. There were black officers who passed over eligible whites who had scored higher on the examination and got promoted in this manner. I had no problem with this method of making up for past discrimination, but I never got promoted in this manner.

There were twenty-seven slots for Sergeant, and I was number three on the eligible list. For Lieutenant I was number two on the list, and there were more than a dozen open slots. Two other blacks were promoted from this list; their names were moved ahead of some eligible whites on that list. I never had to pass over other eligible white officers to get promoted. My name was always close enough to the top and there were enough open positions that my name didn't have to leapfrog any other applicant's. The rank and file whites respected me for this. They had a name for blacks promoted via the Consent Decree: "Welfare Sergeants, Lieutenants, and Captains," because they were given the positions by passing over other eligible white candidates. Suits were filed by some white officers and firemen in regard to this practice. As I recall, the City and federal government prevailed. For over thirty years, some parts of the Consent Decree were in effect against the City of Birmingham and finally came to an end in January 2012.

INTERNAL AFFAIRS ASSIGNMENT EPISODE

After my promotion to Sergeant, I worked as a burglary detective and a patrol supervisor, before being assigned to the Internal Affairs Unit. The primary functions of this unit was to investigate all known allegations of police brutality, misconduct and corruption, as well as to do background investigations on applicants for police positions, conduct interviews with applicants, accused police officers and witnesses, both police and civilians. Prior to and during the late sixties and early seventies, corruption and brutality were widespread within the department. The new Chief, James Parsons, under the direction of the Mayor, was doing his best to eradicate corruption and brutality and foster trust and better relations between the department and the community, by ensuring that the police became more aware of the needs of the community and be more responsive in addressing them.

Each officer was instructed that he was to be a Community Relations Ambassador, a conduit between the department and the community. They were to attend neighborhood meetings in the black and white communities, talk to the leaders, find out what the problems were, and handle them, either directly or by referring them to the proper department to be handled. Every allegation of police corruption or brutality, unlike in the past, was immediately investigated and brought to a conclusion, either by bringing charges against the ones involved or exonerating them.

Either way, the complainant was notified of the results in writing. Many of the hard-liners didn't set well with this concept of community relations, which included police involvement in community affairs. Their idea of policing was to come into a neighborhood and threaten, intimidate, make the necessary arrests and move out, only to return when another so-called police problem was brought to their attention. They spent very little time in the neighborhoods, and they didn't know the leaders and had no dialog with the citizens of the areas, and as a consequence had no knowledge of what went on in the neighborhoods that they were tasked with the responsibility to protect. Their concept of good policing was by intimidation, threats and force. For years, this had been their method for keeping blacks in their place.

It was within this type of climate that I found myself in Internal Affairs. This unit consisted of about six investigators who were Sergeants, with a Lieutenant in charge of the unit. None of the investigators volunteered for the assignment, and most of them didn't want to be there. Internal Affairs, or I.A., was relatively new to our department. The investigators assigned came from the various units within the department. I am not sure all of them were chosen because of their impeccable record regarding corruption and police brutality. With the exception of three, the others wanted nothing to do with investigation of complaints on other officers, which they knew would result in officers being disciplined or fired. They wanted to stay in good fellowship with the rank and file. The Lieutenant whose heart was not into prosecuting other officers did not insist that they be assigned the hard cases that could possibly result in harsh sanctions, including dismissal and or prosecutions.

So that left three other white officers and me to handle the so-called "hard cases."

These three were as straight as an arrow. Investigators usually worked in teams of two when investigating big cases, and investigator D.C. and I were assigned to work together. D.C. "Dudley Do Right," as he was called, and I worked together for close to seven years, during which time we gained the reputation of being tough on crooked cops, but yet fair and impartial. We worked just as hard to clear an officer who was wrongly accused as we did to ensure that the guilty were punished. We were able to make a lot of cases involving officers shaking down shot house operators and motorists, burglarizing businesses, as well as stealing from those previously burglarized prior to calling the owner to the scene.

D.C. and I made numerous cases on officers taking money from shot house operators on their beats. We contacted the operators and gained their trust. This was made easier because I was black, and we asked them for help in getting the crooked officers off the street. We utilized marked money and were very successful. When some arrests were made, the other crooked officers were wary because they didn't know which shot house operators were cooperating with the police. It got to the point where D.C. and I had to check our personal vehicles for explosive devices before we got in them to drive home. I recall an incident where I.A. had received complaints from citizens that a particular officer had been shaking them down for money after stopping them for traffic violations as they passed through his beat. If the citizen refused to pay, the citizen would receive a citation, usually for speeding, running a stop sign or red light. As part of our investigation, we enlisted several citizens to act as pigeons and supplied them with marked money and instructed them to drive through the officer's beat. There were two main arteries on which he usually stopped cars for violations.

On this particular day we had a pigeon drive through the area. In our unmarked car as we were traveling on this main artery, we saw that this particular officer had a car stopped about 3-4 blocks ahead of us. As we got closer, we recognized the vehicle as belonging to our pigeon. The citizen was in the police car. As we got closer, we could see something passed from the citizen's hand to the officer's hand. As we got up almost alongside of the stopped car, the officer recognized us and jumped out of the police car, flagged us down and came up to our car on foot, waving a twenty-dollar bill. He stated to us, "Look what I have! That man gave me a twenty-dollar bill trying to bribe me from giving him a ticket. What do you think that I should do?" I told him, "As a police officer that has a legitimate charge on the driver, do what you would normally do under the circumstances." We took the twenty-dollar bill and D.C. jotted down the serial numbers and gave it back to him and we drove off. Our pigeon later reported that he was not given a ticket. The marked money was returned to him. He stated that the officer appeared to have been scared when he saw us driving up and he jumped out of the car. This officer was ordered to report to I.A. later, where he was confronted with the evidence against him, including other witnesses. His shakedown business was ended once and for all.

Another incident I recall started out routinely enough but almost ended in tragedy. D.C. and I were assigned to investigate a complaint from the City Jail. There was a female black inmate who was in the advanced stage of pregnancy and had been incarcerated for about a year. In other words, the complaint was that she became pregnant while in jail, and that the prospective father of the child was a white police officer. We interviewed the female prisoner in internal affairs, and she told us that the only person she was intimate with since she had been incarcerated was this officer, whose last name was (I'll use the first letter) A. She stated that this officer would come into her cell at night and be intimate with her. In return, he would allow her certain privileges not ordinarily given to other female inmates. We interviewed other witnesses, who confirmed the prisoner's allegations.

Officer A was summoned to Internal Affairs one day after getting off the night shift. He had on his uniform during the interview; we discovered that he had a wife and family. He became very despondent, and we took a break in questioning to allow him to compose himself. D.C. and I were discussing something and had momentarily taken our eyes off officer A. I heard a movement and looked and found that officer A had stood up and was pulling his gun from its holster. I alerted D.C. and we both grabbed the officer and wrestled the gun away from him. He stated that he wasn't trying to harm us; he was trying to kill himself. We really didn't know what his intentions were, but we do know that either way it could have been a disaster. From that time on, we made sure that an officer did not have a gun on his person while being interviewed, whether in uniform or not. As a result of our investigation, officer A was terminated.

The most notable investigation I can recall during my stint in I.A. is what we called the Ensley 15, in that fifteen officers from the Ensley precinct were dismissed from the department for burglary and theft. Truckloads of merchandise taken from various stores and businesses in the Ensley area were recovered. These officers would steal from businesses already broken into before notifying the owners, and they would also break into businesses and stores and help themselves before notifying the owners. During the investigation, we discovered witnesses to both types of occurrences. This investigation was obviously too big for Internal Affairs' Lieutenant E.G, so the department brought in Captain B. R. M., an icon of integrity who didn't condone crooked cops.

He was known as "Booger Red" and he instituted a lot of innovated procedures in order to acquire the necessary evidence for charges to be brought against the perpetrators. One such technique was for Internal Affairs investigators to personally witness intrusions, such as officers entering businesses that had already been burglarized or those that the owners had forgotten to lock their doors. He got several owners to leave their doors unlocked on purpose and have an I. A. investigator staked out within sight of the business in order to observe the rogue officers as they went in and brought items out.

One such business was a grocery market located on Ave. E in Ensley. D.C. and I were given the assignment of covering this location. I was designated to conceal myself as close as possible in a location where I would be able to observe the front door of the business. Along this stretch of street, there were houses as well as businesses, particularly on the side opposite the grocery market. Directly opposite the market was a used car lot, which was the only location where I could have concealment and still be able to observe the unlocked front door of the business. The only way I could see without being seen was to hide under one of the cars parked on the lot. I got in position before the 11-7 shift came on duty. This was the shift where all of the break-ins and thefts had been occurring. D.C. took our unmarked car out of the area, where he monitored his radio in case I needed him. We were on a different channel than the Ensley patrol units.

Sometime before midnight, a patrol unit pulled up in front of the market. One officer got out and checked the door. He found the door to be unlocked and opened the door just a little. The second officer got out and went to the door, but neither one entered the building. They left the door as it was and began looking around the building. After returning from the rear of the building, they both stood in front of the half-opened door but neither went inside. They must have smelled a rat, for it was general knowledge that I.A. was investigating allegations about the Ensley bunch. It could have been someone from I.A. who tipped them off that I.A. was trying to set them up. Everyone that worked in I.A. was not necessarily straight. Whatever the case, they were suspicious and didn't enter the business. One officer pulled the door shut, and they both began walking across the street, shining their flashlights on the houses and the parking lot where I was hiding under a car. As they got closer, I decided that it was time for me to move. I eased out from under the car and, keeping low, moved to the back of the car lot near the alley.

As they went down each row of cars, I knew it would not be long before they would discover me. It would be no telling what they would do. I couldn't take that chance. There was a house across the alley with a fenced-in yard. I kept the last row of cars between the searching officers and I and, staying low, scaled the fence. What I didn't know was there was a dog inside, and he started barking and started after me. I immediately ran to the side of the yard, jumped the fence and started sprinting down the street away from the scene. One of the officers ran to the street from the alley and saw me running from the scene. He yelled to his partner that a black male was running from the scene and it seemed as if he had a police radio. I jumped another yard and went between some houses in case he tried to follow me. I called D. C. on my radio and instructed him to pick me up on Ave. I, some five blocks away. He made the pickup and we got out of there. We didn't need the evidence; I was seeking to make a case against them. As the investigation progressed, they all confessed when confronted with polygraph and fingerprint evidence. Captain "Booger Red" went back to his regular assignment after this investigation was over. The department got rid of fifteen crooked officers as a result of that investigation.

PROMOTION TO LIEUTENANT

After over nine years as a Sergeant, working as a supervisor and investigator, I was promoted to Lieutenant, having attained a score on the exam that placed me in the top three on the eligible promotion list. Two other black sergeants were promoted to Lieutenant at the same time, even though they were much further down on the list. Because of Affirmative Action, they were able to skip over or leapfrog other eligible white officers who scored higher on the promotional examination, and therefore were listed higher on the eligible list for promotion. Since there were only a limited number of slots open for Lieutenant in the department, at least two white eligible applicants did not get promoted, because they were passed over by two black applicants who were much further down on the list. But this was 1982, and because of the Consent Decree between the City and the federal government, Affirmative Action was in full gear, trying to right some of the wrongs blacks suffered in the past in regards to hiring and promotions in the City of Birmingham, in various departments, especially the police.

Of course, this action did not set well with the white officers. A lot of them said that they had no respect for officers promoted in such a manner. Some told me that they respected me and the rank I had obtained, because I had been promoted on my own merit and didn't have to skip over anyone higher on the list in order to get promoted, because there were more than two slots open for Lieutenant in the department. My score enabled me to attain a number two ranking on the eligible list. At that time for that rank, there was no promotional review board in place, and one was promoted in the order in which one's name appeared on the eligible list. Affirmative Action changed all of this by allowing blacks who scored lower on the test, and as a result would be farther down on the eligible list, to leapfrog other applicants who were higher on the list, in order for a quota to be obtained regarding promotion of blacks.

At this time Affirmative Action was also utilized for promotion to Sergeant as well. There was an uproar in the department by white officers concerning this type practice of passing over so-called "more qualified" white applicants to get to a black to fill an open slot for promotion to a particular rank. White officers actually filed a lawsuit in regards to this type of practice. I believe that after several years of compliance by the City, Affirmative Action and the Consent Decree ended. The final ruling on all aspects of this decree was in January 2012.

PROMOTION TO CAPTAIN

Getting promoted to the rank of Captain was another matter. This was a coveted position and highly political. You had to be in the good graces of the higher authority, including the Chief of Police and his inner circle of yes men. Second, at this time the department had instituted a "Promotional Review Board," which interviewed all candidates on the eligibility list. This board would then make its recommendations to the Chief and his inner circle as to which candidates they felt were best suited for the available positions. This had nothing to do with the candidates' positions on the eligible list. It had everything to do with how the powers that be and the Promotional Review Board felt about certain candidates and whether or not they wanted to see them get promoted. It had to do with how well liked they were, and how much the upper echelon wanted to see them promoted.

During all of the examinations that I took for the rank of Captain, my score was such that I always ranked number two or three on the promotional list for that rank. Yet, I was passed over a couple of years by candidates who scored considerably lower on the test, and as a result were ranked lower on the eligibility list. To compound matters, I was not only skipped over by whites, but by a couple of blacks and a white female who better fit into their scheme of things. I didn't let this deter me, for every time the test was given I was right there, and I always scored high enough to be placed in the top three on the eligible list for Captain. I didn't gripe or sulk, but continued to do my job in a professional manner.

After a couple of years of being passed over, one of my friends who was a police officer pulled the black Mayor's coattail about what was happening. Word got around that the Mayor was investigating the situation, and the wheels started turning in my favor. The last examination I took for the position of Captain, my score was high enough that I was number two on the eligible list. This time around I was recommended for promotion, and to my surprise I was promoted. It was God that prompted my friends to contact the Mayor on my behalf, and God who touched the Mayor's heart to put pressure on the Chief and his henchmen to do the right thing. The rank of Captain in the Birmingham Police Department is the highest rank that one can attain through promotional examination. All ranks above Captain are appointed positions. At one time, we had an Inspector as well as a Deputy Chief position. The position of Inspector was later eliminated and only the rank of Deputy Chief remained.

PROMOTION TO CAPTAIN AND WEST PRECINCT COMMANDER

As a Captain, I was assigned as West Precinct Commander by Deputy Chief Newfield, who said that he wanted me to, as he put it, "straighten the precinct out." In the beginning, I let it be known that I expected a full day's work for a day's pay. I let it be known that I expected a full cup and nothing less. I became known as the "Full Cup" Commander. I utilized praise and recognition for a job well done, and discipline where needed as a last resort. All of the officers were encouraged to see me at anytime about anything, with permission from their supervisor, and if permission was refused, to let me know.

During my tenure, morale and productivity dramatically improved and the 'West Precinct became known as the "Best Precinct." After such improvement at the West Precinct, Deputy Chief Newfield sent me to the North Precinct, which, as he said, was in need of "straightening out." The citizens and officers didn't want to see me leave the West Precinct. I had established a good relationship with the community and neighborhood leaders through the beat officers, supervisors and myself attending all meetings with our crime prevention officer, listening to their complaints, recording them and addressing them and reporting back to them as to how they had been handled. I instituted a walk and talk program, where beat officers would park their cars, get out and walk the neighborhood and talk to the citizens. I also utilized what we called "good morning cards," which the officers on the night shift would place in the doors of businesses to let the owner or operators know that their business had been checked during the night. I also instituted the "Better City Services Sergeant" program, where citizens could call in complaints about pot holes, weeds, abandoned houses, vagrants, drugs or any other problem they were aware of to the precinct, and an officer would record their complaints and a Sergeant would refer the citizens' complaints to the particular City department or unit that had responsibility for handling such complaints. The citizens had complained to me about how they had called in complaints about particular problems to the responsible City departments and would get no response or be given the runaround. The citizens saw the difference in response to their complaints and were very appreciative of what we were doing on their behalf.

DEPUTY CHIEF LEROY STOVER, RETIRED

Shiloh Hi News and Views

VOL. I.   SARDIS, ALABAMA, December, 1951   NUMBER 1.

OUR SCHOOL'S HISTORY
By Mrs. G. D. Allen

Located on a red clay hill two miles west of Sardis you will see one of the most modern schools in the State of Alabama. This is Shiloh High School.

Shiloh was started during the latter part of the 19th century in a little one-room log cabin about one hundred feet from where the present school now stands. The school had one teacher for a number of years and carried grades 1-6. Among the earlier teachers were Mrs. Towns, and later Mr. John Rivers, who taught from 1907-09.

Around 1920, Mr. Rickstraw, a representative for the Julius Rosenwald Fund came into the community and so aroused the thirst for better schools and better education that they raised funds (each family paying $10.00) to build the school. The people raised $650.00 which was matched by the Rosenwald Fund. This building (which is still a part of our school) was completed in 1923.

The first teachers in this school were Mr. Lawrence Johnson and Miss Cornelia Jackson who is now Mrs. Cornelia Glover and still a member of our teaching force. The school has been enlarged through the persistent efforts of the parents, teachers, and school board.

In the year 1938, Mr. James Dixon came to be the principal of the school, now a three teacher school. The school was raised to a Junior High School under his administration.

Mr. I. T. Martin was made principal in 1932 and served for 12 years. Through his efforts and with the help of the present P. T. A., the school was made larger, more rooms added, Home Economics and Basketball were added and the grounds were beautified. The school then

LEROY STOVER, Editor

A ranking student of Senior III Class and affiliated with the Hi-Y Club, Chorus, Dramatic Club, active in all athletics, and treasurer of his class.

carried seven grades and twelve teacher.

After several other administrations, Mr. B. F. Baynes was appointed principal in 1946. Under his administration the teaching has grown to fourteen with an enrollment of over 450 students. We now have a complete high school with Music, Physical Education, Commercial Arts, and Athletics. The boys and girls are able to participate in such clubs as the Y-Teen, Hi-Y, Dramatic Club, Choral groups, Basketball and Softball. The buildings are three in number. One for primary department, one for elementary and a modern 11-room brick building for the high school department. This new building was completed in October, 1949. The aim of the principal and teachers is to "Build a Better Community Through Our Youth."

PTA NEWS

The PTA met recently with a hold over of all officers of last year.
Mrs. Elizabeth Moore ____ President
Mrs. Brooks Dembo _ Vice President
Mrs. A. James ____ Secretary
Mrs. C. Glover ____ Asst. Secretary
Mrs. Pauline Barnes ____ Treasurer

We have a majority of old members back, and a number of new ones.

These are the persons on whose shoulders rest the greatest responsibility of living up to a great name established by the PTA's of past years. They are resolved to excell in all efforts.

Y-TEEN NEWS
By Rosa M. Ford

The Y-Teen Club was reorganized for the year during the month of October. The officers of the club are:
Rose Mary Ford ____ President
Eloise Wilson ____ Vice President
Margaret Holyfield ____ Secretary
Roberta Glover ____ Treasurer
Mrs. M. L. Upshaw, Mrs. G. D. Allen, ____ Advisors

The girls are still following our Y-Teen purpose which is Building Better Womanhood. We are still working toward projects similar to those of past years.

CHORUS NEWS

The school chorus, under the direction of Mr. W. J. Mills is progressing nicely and leaving no loopholes in preparation for their concert to be given on December 19, 1951 in the school auditorium.

Did you know the enrollment at Shiloh has increased over 100 percent in two years?

BIRMINGHAM'S FIRST BLACK IN BLUE

NEW YORK, March 30—(P)—The FBI arrested 38 men in daybreak raids today and said they have cracked ... New York and Cleveland ... e enlistment papers for up

City hires first Negro policeman

Police Chief Jamie Moore today announced the hiring of the first Birmingham Negro police officer and indicated that a second will probably be employed Thursday.

The first of his race to join the Birmingham Police Department, effective today, is Leroy Stover, 33, of 45 Ninth Ave. North.

Birmingham Police Chief Jamie Moore, Retired

DEPUTY CHIEF LEROY STOVER, RETIRED

Employee mugshot taken on 3/17/66, Leroy Stover

BIRMINGHAM'S FIRST BLACK IN BLUE

Deputy Chief Leroy Stover, left, and Sgt. LaFaree King-Walker, right, lead police choir.

Onward Christian soldiers
Birmingham police gospel choir raises voice to spread harmony

By **Roy Williams**
News staff writer

"Glory! glory, hallelujah! His truth is marching on."

The choir members singing those words during a recent practice session not only consider themselves Christian soldiers, but soldiers in Birmingham's war against crime.

They make up the Birmingham Police Department Gospel Choir, a 15-member group of police officers, secretaries and a deputy police chief who combine their voices to spread God's message of love through song.

The choir, formed in December, includes Deputy Chief Leroy Stover, an original member of the Friendly Four, a Selma-based gospel group popular in the 1950s.

Public Information Officer Sgt. LaFaree King-Walker, a featured soloist in the church choir at Trinity AME Zion Church in Ensley, is the group's director.

"We're using this as an opportunity to show the lighter side or flip side of policing," she said.

"People often think of police as unfeeling, cold-hearted. We have as many feelings and are as Christian-hearted as the next person. We use this as an opportunity to express ourselves."

The choir was formed shortly before Christmas when acting chief Johnnie Johnson requested some officers get together to sing carols at the Ketona Nursing Home, Sgt. King-Walker said.

"The officers liked it so much they expressed a desire to sing together more often," she said.

The choir practices every month at Trinity AME Zion Church, Sgt. King-Walker said. "Our pastor, the Rev. Thomas F. Felder, has been gracious in allowing us to practice there," she said.

The choir welcomes opportunities to perform for the public, Sgt. King-Walker said. "We'll go anywhere we're invited to, as long as our musicians are available," she said.

On June 6, the choir performed a memorial service honoring John Huffman, the Birmingham officer struck and killed last month by a car driven by a suspected drunken driver.

The performance was the choir's

See **Choir**, Page **2G**

The Birmingham Police Choir

DEPUTY CHIEF LEROY STOVER, RETIRED

1952, Leroy Stover 82nd Airborne DIV

1953 - 1955, Leroy Stover 187th Airborne R.C.T.

DEPUTY CHIEF LEROY STOVER, RETIRED

Paratrooper Leroy and Robert Stover

*Leroy Stover on graduation day from the
University of Alabama, Birmingham (UA.B.), June 1976*

Lt. Leroy Stover at the East Precinct

Awards ceremony at City Hall

DEPUTY CHIEF LEROY STOVER, RETIRED

Another game at the park

Stover playing softball

BIRMINGHAM'S FIRST BLACK IN BLUE

Stover Family
Mr. Albert Stover, Mrs. Georgia Ramsey, Mr. Leroy Stover, Mr. Mose Stover, Sr., Mrs. Bessie E. Stover, Mr. Robert Stover, Mrs. Josephine Wallace, Mr. Mose Stover, Jr., and Mr. Norman Stover

Our wedding day July 20, 1991
Mrs. Joe Ann Stover, Deputy Chief Leroy Stover, Mrs. Sophronia Oden, Pastor Ocie Oden Jr.

DEPUTY CHIEF LEROY STOVER, RETIRED

Stover Family at Whitehall, AL

Ms. Kandice Stover, grand daugther and Deputy Chief Leroy Stover

*1990 The old Antioch church on 54th St. Fairfield, Alabama
Deacon James Oden, Deacon Ocie Oden, Sr., Deacon Leroy Stover*

DEPUTY CHIEF LEROY STOVER, RETIRED

Deputy Chief Stover visiting local Birmingham schools

Deputy Chief Stover visiting local Birmingham schools

BIRMINGHAM'S FIRST BLACK IN BLUE

Deputy Chief Stover visiting local Birmingham schools

Deputy Chief Stover visiting local Birmingham schools

DEPUTY CHIEF LEROY STOVER, RETIRED

Deputy Chief Leroy Stover on his way to work

*Deputy Chief Leroy Stover, Mrs. Wilma Herring,
Former Secretary North Precinct*

BIRMINGHAM'S FIRST BLACK IN BLUE

Office Staff: Mrs. Henrietta Henderson, Capt. Cructhfield, Deputy Chief Leroy Stover. Lt. Roy Williams, Sgt. Patricia King

Former Birmingham Police Chief Jamie Moore, Deputy Chief Leroy Stover

DEPUTY CHIEF LEROY STOVER, RETIRED

Police Academy
City of Birmingham
Certificate of Graduation

This is to Certify that LEROY STOVER has completed the general course of instruction prescribed in The Police Academy of the City of Birmingham and is hereby awarded this Certificate of Proficiency.

Dated at Birmingham, Alabama this 1st day of December 19 66

Mayor

Jamie Moore, Chief of Police

A copy of Deputy Chief Leroy Stover's Birmingham Police Academy certificate of graduation dated December 1, 1966

BIRMINGHAM'S FIRST BLACK IN BLUE

The University of Alabama in Birmingham

By authority of the Board of Trustees
on the recommendation of the faculty of the
School of Social and Behavioral Science
the degree

Bachelor of Science

with all the accompanying rights and privileges
has been conferred upon

Leroy Stover

In Testimony Whereof, this diploma is issued with the seal of the University
and the signatures authorized by the Trustees hereunto affixed.

Given at the University in Birmingham on the sixth day of June, 1976.

A copy of Deputy Chief Leroy Stover's diploma from the University of Alabama in Birmingham (U.A.B.)

DEPUTY CHIEF LEROY STOVER, RETIRED

Deputy Chief Leroy Stover

BIRMINGHAM'S FIRST BLACK IN BLUE

Deputy Chief Leroy Stover, Retired

DEPUTY CHIEF LEROY STOVER, RETIRED

JUST A CHAT

. . . with Capt. Leroy Stover

Occupation: Commander of the Birmingham Police Department's North Precinct.

Age: 54.

Residence: West End Manor.

If I didn't have this job, I'd want to be a: Fireman. When I was a kid, I'd see these firetrucks going by. It was kind of exciting.

My biggest accomplishment has been: Being able to move through the ranks to the position I now have, and my work with my church. I'm chairman of the board of deacons at Antioch Baptist Church in Fairfield.

The last thing I really messed up on was: A long time ago, in 1952, when I volunteered for the military on a dare with my friends. They didn't show up at the recruiting station and I did. I couldn't chicken out. Nobody was there but me. I was a paratrooper in the Army for three years. I'm glad of it now. It was good experience.

If I got $1 million tomorrow, I'd: Give some to my church, and help out some needy causes. I'd save enough to live comfortably myself.

My favorite TV show is: *Matlock*.

My favorite movie is: *Rainman*.

My favorite musical groups are: The Platters and the Drifters.

My favorite junk food is: Ice cream and cookies.

If I were an animal, I'd want to be a: Lion.

What most people don't know about me is: I'm really concerned about humanity. I have a soft spot for the underdogs, so to speak, the down-and-out.

The best advice my parents ever gave me was: Tell the truth, and don't cheat or steal. Treat people like you'd like to be treated.

My best childhood memory is: My camaraderie with my six sisters and brothers. My brothers and I used to go swimming all the time in a creek not far from where we lived in Dallas County.

If I could travel in a time machine, I'd go: Back to Africa in the years prior to our ancestors coming over here, to see what it was like back then, to see my roots.

The biggest problem facing the world today is: The inability of world leadership to reach a consensus on problems dealing with different ideologies and human rights, like communism vs. capitalism.

— *Bryan Crowson*

NORTH PRECINCT COMMANDER I
PROMOTION TO DEPUTY CHIEF I RETIREMENT

After being transferred to the North Precinct, I let it be known that I would not tolerate corruption, brutality or maltreatment of citizens. I let it be known that if they did their job to the best of their ability, they would have no problem from me. I instituted some of the same programs that were working in the West Precinct. I also allowed several neighborhoods to hold meetings at the precinct because we had plenty of room. I also instituted a bicycle program. The bicycle unit patrolled the downtown business district, including the Civic Center area. I also had six officers and a supervisor who actually walked the business area of downtown to protect the thousands of citizens who converge on the downtown area during weekdays and in particular during lunchtime, when employees from the various businesses flocked to the various eating establishments downtown.

    I was at the North Precinct until I was promoted to Deputy Chief of Field Operations. After several years as Commander of two different precincts, an unusual turn of events occurred that eventually catapulted me into the Deputy Chief position. My wife and I had been on vacation for a couple of weeks, and when we returned, I found out that my old nemesis Chief A. D. was out, resigned, retired or whatever, and the Mayor had appointed Johnnie Johnson, the second black police officer hired by the department, to the position of Chief. With the Mayor's concurrence, Johnnie selected me to become Deputy Chief in charge of the uniform division (Patrol), or Field Operations, replacing Charles Newfield, a white officer, who took over the detective division.

Under this leadership, all categories of crime decreased dramatically with the exception of homicides for several years. Deputy Chief Newfield retired and the Chief replaced him with another white officer as Deputy Chief. Finally, after six to seven years, the Chief and the Mayor began to be at odds over certain issues and the Chief retired and the Mayor replaced him with a white Captain from the East Precinct, one who was popular with the white community. The top brass in the police department and other City departments had become top heavy with blacks. The police department had a black Chief and three black Deputy Chiefs, with only one white Deputy Chief. There was similar type representation in the various precincts and units throughout the department. This type of configuration did not sit well with the white business sector, which controlled the money in Birmingham.

Various departments with such a large percentage of black department heads, and in particular the fire and police, were becoming too black. With pressure from the white community and businesses, it was expedient for the Mayor to get rid of the Black Chief and replace him with a white who was popular with the white constituents in the eastern section, and white businesses in general. With a white Chief of Police in Birmingham, this could have been their great White Hope, and from the Mayor's perspective might just have slowed down the "White Flight" from the city, thus stabilizing the tax base. The position of Chief and Deputy Chief are highly political and are at the whim of the Mayor and politicians in the city at the time. The tenure of Chief is also at the whim of this political structure. A police chief's tenure average is about four to seven years, unless the administration changes before then and the new Mayor decides to get his own Chief, then it is considerably shorter.

The new Chief and I did not see eye-to-eye on several issues regarding management in the East Precinct (while he was a Captain). I had called him in on a few occasions regarding problems concerning black personnel at his precinct that had come to my attention. There was no love lost between the two of us. When he came on board, he let it be known how he felt. I am a professional. I don't buck those in authority; so I decided that it was time for me to move on to retire, go out on top. Hundreds of officers begged me not to leave, but I felt in my heart that the time was right. So I retired, having spent thirty-two years with the department. Sometime later the Mayor abdicated the position of Mayor, and not long after that the new Chief retired and went on to other things.

My career with the Birmingham Police Department spanned over three decades and I don't regret one single day of that time. God placed me in the position to be the first black to integrate the all-white department. God was with me every step of my journey as a Birmingham policeman. He protected and directed my steps, opening doors for me as I moved up through the ranks. God made my enemies behave and touched the hearts of those that reached out and assisted me on my journey. My heartfelt appreciation goes out to Chief Jamie Moore, who despite his gruff exterior was truly a good friend, who was always looking out for my welfare. He would ride out on the beat that I was working on to ensure that the white officers I was assigned with were treating me fairly.

After I was promoted to higher ranks, Chief Moore would call me two or three times a week. After I retired, we would talk regularly by telephone up until he passed. He once told me that back in 1956, he requested that the city hire colored officers. He told me that if I didn't believe it, to check the newspapers for that year. I went to the library and checked the *Birmingham News* and found to my surprise that on May 28, 1963, the paper had printed an article that said Chief Jamie Moore back in 1956 had vowed to someday "Hire a Negro officer."[1]

He was very pleased when I told him that I had found the article. He told me that he saw a need for colored police, but his hands were tied under Bull Connor's regime. Another supporter was Deputy Chief Jack Warren, whom I got to know from my involvement in Civil Defense. This was the only unit blacks could belong to that allowed them to carry firearms while on duty only. This was the closest thing to a police officer a black could be engaged in. Our Commander, Chief Warren, was white. He conducted the background investigation on me prior to my being hired. He was a military man, a member of the National Guard. He was a gentleman and true friend who assisted me throughout my career. Chief Bill Myers was real helpful in furthering my career. He was truly concerned with my welfare and did everything possible to assist me in my development as an officer. I mention these three, but there were others too numerous to mention that assisted me in my development as an officer with the Birmingham Police Department.

My hiring as the first black police officer in the all-white Police Department did not just happen overnight, nor was it the brainchild of any one individual, who having come up with the idea was solely responsible for pushing it through to fruition. It was much more than that: it was the culmination of sacrifices and hard work on the part of diverse individuals small and great who struggled for individual and civil rights, who endured hardships and persecutions, such as beatings, and sometimes lost their lives in their quest for equal rights and representation in all facets of society due to American citizens as guaranteed under the Constitution of the United States. It states in part: that all men are created equal; they are endowed by their creator with certain inalienable rights; among

---

[1] *Birmingham News,* May 28, 1963

these are life, liberty and the pursuit of happiness. It was the involvement of civil rights groups who organized non-violent protests, marches and sit-ins at businesses to protest their racial practices of excluding blacks. The leaders and participants endured beatings by racist police: biting by vicious police dogs, being knocked down by fire hoses and even thrown in jail because they were able to come together and engage in dialogue with one another and come to the conclusion that Birmingham under Bull Connor was heading in a direction that was not in the best interest of all of its citizens, and that a change had to be made. The change came about when the City voted the Commission out of office and voted in a Mayor Council form of government, even though the Commission hung around for about six months. As a result of this change, blacks were eventually incorporated into various city departments that were previously all white, thus paving the way for that historical event that took place on March 30, 1966, when I became Birmingham's first black police officer.

I would be remiss if I didn't mention some unsung heroes that were involved in furthering my career and making my tenure as Precinct and Field Operations Commander fruitful and enjoyable endeavors: hard-working, efficient secretaries, clerical and administrative personnel keep any organization running smoothly. I believe that I was blessed with the best personnel available in the department. At the West Precinct there was Mrs. Dot, Secretary, and Shift Commanders and Supervisors. At the North Precinct there was Mrs. Wilma Herring, Secretary, and the Shift Commanders and Supervisors, and in the Deputy Chief's office there was Mrs. Henrietta, the most hard-working person I have ever seen, along with Pat and Glenda. Captain Trucks was invaluable in his assistance and expertise. Captain Crutchfield was helpful, and Lieutenant Roy Williams gave spiritual support. The last three didn't stay with me in the Deputy Chief's office for very long, but were transferred to other assignments. The core group of Mrs. Henrietta Henderson, Patricia King and Glenda Dunklin were with me until I retired. For a long time they were the only administrative personnel I had in the office. They did the work of a Captain and Lieutenant. They were my Administrative Assistants, and with their help we kept the office running smoothly, administering to the uniform personnel.

BIRMINGHAM'S FIRST BLACK IN BLUE

▶ BIRMINGHAM 1998

First black police officer retiring

By Lewis Kamb
Birmingham Post-Herald

When 33-year-old Leroy Stover stepped into City Hall on March 30, 1966, to receive badge number 65 and a pistol, the haunting images of a police force under the commands of the notorious Bull Connor remained fresh in the American consciousness.

But as the first black to break into the ranks of an all-white force, Stover brought the Birmingham Police Department into a new era.

On Thursday, the department announced that after nearly 32 years of service, Deputy Chief Stover is retiring. He will be honored today between 2 and 3:30 p.m. at the Birmingham Police Academy.

Although Stover could not be reached for comment, former police chief and long-time friend Johnnie Johnson said he spoke with Stover about his future Thursday morning.

"He said things are pretty much wide open for him right now," Johnson said. "Anything's possible for him."

That may be an understatement.

The son of a Dallas County sharecropper, Stover was a pioneer of sorts long before he carried a badge. After graduating from Shiloh High School in Selma in the early 1950s, he joined the U.S. Army and became a paratrooper first with the 82nd Airborne, then in the last year of the Korean War in 1952-53 with the 187th Airborne Regimental Combat Team. Stover completed more than 78 jumps before leaving the service in 1959 to take a job in Birmingham.

Stover was a married father of two children who drove a truck for a Pratt City construction company when he took and passed the civil service exam in 1966.

"Several blacks had passed the test by then, including a professor from Miles College, but the city always found reasons to not hire them," Stover told the Post-Herald in 1991.

"I guess the difference with me was that there was no civil rights activist pushing for me. That apparently made me a little easier for them to take."

A Birmingham Post-Herald article dated March 31, 1966, documented the historic hiring as Stover showed up for his first day on the job. "He (Stover) was sneaked into City Hall and was kept away from photographers who were anxious to get a picture of a big first in Birmingham," the article said.

Then-Capt. Glen V. Evans of the department's Uniformed Division traveled throughout the department to inform officers on all shifts of Stover's hiring, the article reported. Evans told the officers that Stover would be treated with the same respect, wear the same type of uniform, receive the same pay, perform the same duties and wield the same authority as other officers of his rank.

"The only difference will be the difference in the color of the skin," Evans was then quoted as saying.

But Johnson, who became Birmingham's second black officer the day after Stover was hired, said that it wasn't quite how he remembers his and Stover's first days.

Please turn to RETIRE, page A5

File photo
Leroy Stover, the first black officer in the Birmingham Police Department, is retiring after almost 32 years. He joined the department in March 1966.

MY REFLECTIONS ON THE CRIMINAL JUSTICE SYSTEM

The Police, the Courts and Corrections:

The Police is tasked with protection, service and apprehension of those charged with a crime.

The Courts' duty is to try those charged with a crime and prosecute those found guilty, so that justice may be served, keeping in mind that fairness and the idea that a defendant must be considered innocent until such time as proven guilty in a court of law.

Corrections is tasked with incarceration, rehabilitation, probation and/or parole.

For the criminal justice system to be a viable, effective organism, it must operate on the premise that a defendant must be considered innocent until proven guilty in court. There can be no place for prejudice, bias or preconceived notions regarding a person's guilt or innocence based on a person's race, creed, national origin or station in life. This has to start with the police.

As a police officer in the City of Birmingham, I operated under this system for about thirty-two years. During this time I experienced the good, the bad, as well as the ugly as it evolved over the years to what it is today. In the police arena, I witnessed in past years what we now know as racial profiling at its worse, as blacks were singled out for citations and arrest, sometimes when the only obvious violation or crime was their ethnicity. During my early years I became aware of flagrant corruption by certain white officers as they preyed on known black law violators. However, over time, with better training and the ability of law enforcement to police itself and weed out some of the bad eggs, a more professional officer emerged over the years who concentrated more on the offense committed rather than on the ethnicity of the offender involved.

In the municipal courts in my early years in the department, the arresting officer presented the case and acted as prosecutor before the municipal judge. In most misdemeanor cases, a city attorney was almost non-existent except those that were set for trial. In those cases where the police officer acted as prosecutor and presented the case to the municipal judge, in over ninety-nine percent of cases, the judge ruled with the officer and against the defendant. In the cases that were tried in both municipal and circuit court, plea bargaining was the rule rather than the exception. Smart lawyers used this device to secure lighter sentences for their clients. It was also utilized by some judges to help clear the court docket of cases. The three strike rule, where a defendant that accrued three felony convictions was sentenced to life without parole, had its good and bad points. The good was that it got some bad eggs off the streets for good, such as robbers, drug dealers, and those who had committed felony assaults or sex offenders. On the other hand, there were those who were incarcerated for life without parole who had committed no violent or drug-related crimes but committed three felonies nevertheless. My thoughts are that maybe the courts should use some method to differentiate between violent and non-violent violators who have three felony convictions, and that instead of a blanket life without parole for all offenders that falls into that category, that some sort of sentencing guidelines could be instituted commensurate with the severity of the three felony convictions. This could entail changing or modifying the current three strike law now in effect.

I know of an individual who was the victim of the three strike law whose felony convictions were neither violent, nor sex offenses or drug related. When I was a rookie officer, he was an equal rights activist and an outspoken critic of police brutality. He happened to be black, and it seemed that every time a white policeman saw him, he was arrested for one thing or another, both misdemeanors and felonies. When he had accumulated three felony convictions, he was incarcerated for life. He has been in prison for at least forty years if he is still alive. I can't judge the validity of the charges against him; I just put it out there for your information as it relates to the three strikes and out law.

During my early years in law enforcement, I found that corrections fell far short of its intended goal of security and training development of the individual. Security was great once a prisoner was remanded to prison—his chances for escape were slim to none. Prisons did a great job of protecting the public from those incarcerated. I found that there was little to no training and development of the individual to make it easier for him to assimilate back into society as an asset rather than a liability. Most prisons served as warehouses, keeping the prisoners secure from the public, if not from themselves. There was little training or development involved. They were kept secure until such time as they were released on parole, served their full time or died in prison. Fortunately, this has changed over time, as prisons now have many types of training programs for inmates.

They offer education programs where the GED and other degrees can be earned and trades can be learned, thus enabling inmates to become productive members of society once they are released from prison. Prisons instituted work release programs, where eligible inmates lived and worked outside the prisons at regular jobs. There are some prisons that have inmates that talk to young people about crime and its negative effects. I realize that our criminal justice system is not perfect, but it's the best system in the world. I gained valuable experience operating within this system for over thirty years as to how the three entities operate and how they are interrelated to each other. When all are working as they should, the system will continue to operate smoothly, but when even one component of the system fails to operate as it should, there is chaos and the whole system suffers as a result.

DEPUTY CHIEF LEROY STOVER, RETIRED

*From left to right – Birmingham Police Chief A.C. Roper,
Deputy Chief Leroy Stover and Sgt. Brian Shelton.
Stover's recent visit to the South Precinct on February 28, 2014.*

CONCLUSION

Whatever success I had as Field Operations Commander, I owe it all to the cadre of personnel working behind the scenes, away from the spotlight, doing an incredible job day in and day out to insure that the goals and objectives of the Field Operations Bureau and the Police Department were carried out. My heartfelt thanks goes out to everyone, from the officers on the beat to the supervisors and commanders for a job well done in helping me to become the best that I could be. Thanks for your faith and trust in me over the years. You were like family to me. I'll always remember and cherish the time we spent together, making our part of the world a better place for all we came in contact with.

ABOUT THE AUTHOR

Deputy Chief Leroy Stover, Retired, was born and raised in Dallas County in Sardis, Alabama. His greatest ambition was to finish high school, leave the farm, and get a job at U.S. Steel in Birmingham like his father and two older brothers.

After excelling in three sports, serving as the editor for his school's newspaper, and graduating as the valedictorian of Shiloh High School, the author enlisted to serve in the Korean War rather than waiting to be drafted. He served with the 82nd Airborne Division, as well as the 187 Airborne RCT in Korean and Japan.

Despite rampant racism, the author scored incredibly high on the entrance exam, and was hired as the first Black Policeman in Birmingham, Alabama. He went on to expose the unfair treatment of Black Americans at the hands of bigoted police officers, and worked to improve conditions from the inside.

The author would like to thank his wife, Joe Ann Stover, his friends and co-workers Rev. Larry McMillian, John Fisher, Johnnie Johnson, Jr., and Robert Boswell.

He is a member of the Antioch Missionary Baptist Church in Fairfield, Alabama. His pastor is Dr. O.C. Oden Jr.. Stover serves as leader of the deacon ministry and teaches a class on Christian discipleship. He enjoys working on classic cars and gardening. His motto is John 9:4 which says, I must work the works of Him that sent me, while it is day; for night comes when no man can work. ("Do all you can while you can.")

CPSIA information can be obtained
at www.ICGtesting.com
Printed in the USA
LVOW12s1008121117
555989LV00004B/361/P